# TINY'S WALL

God bless yal!

FRAN "TINY" FIDLER

PSALM 94: 17-19

# TINY'S WALL

A True Story of One Man's Battle
to Overcome the Shame
of Childhood Sexual Abuse

## FRAN FIDLER

WWW.TINYSWALL.COM

Tiny's Wall

*A True Story of One Man's Battle to*
*Overcome the Shame of Childhood Sexual Abuse*

Fran Fidler

FIRST EDITION

ISBN: 978-0-692-04000-3
eBook ISBN: 978-0-692-04401-0
Audio Book ISBN: 978-0-578-41629-8

Library of Congress Control Number: 2018911703

This memoir is a work of creative nonfiction.
The events are portrayed to the best of the author's memory.
While all the stories in this book are true, neither the author
nor Mustard Seed Writing make any representations as to the accuracy
of the events portrayed herein.

Mustard Seed Writing

# FOREWORD

Back in 1982, I directed my very first race, a triathlon called the Bay State Triathlon at Spot Pond in my hometown of Medford. Fran Fidler was a participant. At the time, I was also managing the Saucony Triathlon Team. I didn't know Fran then, but in 1983 I met him at the Tufts 10K for Women where he was hanging around the finish line waiting to talk to me. All I knew about him was that he did my triathlon the year before. There he was, waiting nervously to meet me. Of course I didn't know he had a stutter or how hard it was for him at times to even introduce himself. He asked me what the criteria was to be a sponsored athlete of the Saucony team. I explained to him that there were different levels of sponsorship and asked him if he was interested in being a member of the team. He was thrilled to be asked and graciously accepted the offer.

Fran was on the team in 1985 and 1986. He competed in numerous triathlons throughout the New England area and even volunteered where and when he could. Unfortunately, in August of 1985, he was hit by a car while cycling. The collision could easily have been fatal. As it was, Fran broke his humerus bone. It was his first time ever with a serious injury, but he worked his way back into great shape, and in June of 1986 he won the Equalizer, a local triathlon which consisted of a four-mile swim, a fifty-five-mile bike ride, and a fifteen-mile run. Fran then committed to doing the granddaddy of all triathlons—the Hawaii Ironman. Fran's friends had a fundraising event at the Boston Athletic Club to help him fund the trip.

As I have since learned, and as you will learn in reading this book, Fran's journey after returning home from the Ironman was anything but celebratory. But what has always impressed me the most about

Fran is his perseverance and his commitment to overcoming obstacles, even a few self-inflicted ones. He has always tried his best to be a good person, a good father, a good husband, and a good friend. Through the years, our friendship has developed into one of caring and mutual respect.

In 2002, Fran invited me to a running event, Hope for Children 10K, in Naples, Florida. It was an event he created in the hopes of bringing more awareness to numerous children's causes, especially the healing and recovery of young boys and adult men from the ravages of childhood abuse. I was impressed and touched by Fran's caring and concern for children in need. It was then that I realized Fran and I had so much in common and that our past stories were very similar and would continue to be so in the future.

In 2006, I wrote a book called *The Last Pick.* From time to time, Fran would mention to me that he, too, was writing a book chronicling his childhood and how he, too, had to overcome obstacles.

Then in October of 2013, finding myself short of breath on my runs, I was diagnosed with coronary artery disease. I had some testing done, but early tests indicated no trouble. Further tests were taken and I was told that I had multiple blockages and a narrowing in a number of my arteries.

Fran, as it would happen, would suffer similar breathing issues at the 2015 St. Anthony's Triathlon in Tampa, and then at a local sprint triathlon in Naples. So began his testing. We kept in close touch about our similar health challenges. Fran then went to Mass General Hospital in Boston, the same hospital where I was treated. He returned to Naples, Florida, with more tests scheduled, and it was then determined that a new aortic valve would be necessary.

As expected with the long and arduous recovery from open-heart surgery, Fran did the work to come back at a much slower pace. There were some bumps in the road as he hoped to again find some competitiveness within himself. In 2016, Fran drove out to Boulder, Colorado. While en route, he experienced racing of the heart one night and crazy thoughts ran through his mind. He made it to Boulder, participated in an Olympic distance triathlon, and the next day saw some doctors. The athletic hopes that Fran had on his way to Colorado were now replaced by doctor's appointments, more tests, various medications, and eventually a spinal tap to look for causes of severe headaches, as well as to ensure that there was no internal bleeding. As always, Fran and I talked several times about what he was experiencing and how to best cope with all of it.

During a routine swim practice in December of 2016, Fran suffered severe left arm pain which extended into his neck and back. Though the pain subsided once he was at the emergency room, the hospital thought it was best to keep him for three days. After extensive testing, they found nothing wrong. But during that three-day stay, that still, inner voice many of us often hear but sometimes ignore came to say that he should finish the book he'd started so long ago. Through many self doubts and much disbelief in his ability to not only write such a difficult book, but to follow through and share his pain and shame with us, the readers, Fran chose this time to listen to that voice, understanding that it was no longer about himself. The book, he realized, could possibly help someone else.

He sought the help necessary to make his writings readable and produced this amazing book about overcoming obstacles of every kind. I know that you will be inspired and encouraged by it. Following Fran's humble journey along his path of healing and redemption, you might cry at parts, and at times become angry. "Somebody's got to help that boy," you may find yourself saying. And then you might laugh as Fran has had the opportunity to laugh at himself, albeit mostly in the rearview mirror. In the end, you'll discover that the highs and lows of the journey, the encouragements and discouragements, and the failures and successes are well worth the trip.

So here is Fran now—at the start of a new journey. He's still out there, volunteering when and where possible, still swimming, still cycling, still running, and still working. More importantly, he's still being a good dad, a good husband, and a really good friend. May you, too, shout from the top of your lungs when finished: "Atta boy, Fran! Good job!"

## Dave McGillivray, August, 2018

About Dave McGillivray: Dave is a race director, philanthropist, motivational speaker, and athlete. He's run more than 150,000 miles, most of which have been for charity, raising millions for worthy causes. He's completed 155 marathons. Personal bests: marathon, 2:29:58; Ironman, 10:36:42. Since 1981 Dave has owned and operated DMSE Sports and has organized or consulted on more than 1,000 events, raising millions for charity and earning a reputation for his company as one of the most thorough, well-organized race management firms in the United States. More on Dave can be found at (*https://www.dmsesports.com/*).

# A NOTE TO THE READER

I understand this will be a difficult read for many. The subject matter is tough enough. And then there are those *four-letter words*. As much as I would have liked to have used other words (oh gosh, by golly, geez, gee wiz), that just wasn't the way it was. In this endeavor to help others, as well as to continue my own healing journey, I've tried to be completely honest and transparent, and this includes the exposure of many of my own faults, mistakes, and shortcomings.

I often thought of myself as a coward for waiting so long to write about this. But it's been shared with me that the difference between courageous people and cowardly people is not the lack of fear in the former. The difference is that the courageous people act despite their fear. And so I began to write.

As often as I say I pray, and ask for help, guidance, and direction, I have found my "rock-solid" faith often comes and goes. Yes, I had my reasons but I struggle to understand the doubting of my faith and the doubting of my own voice for such a long time. My outward appearance rarely matched the tumultuous battle between my ears, the repeated beatings of my own self and self worth.

Not that I didn't have my coping strategies. I tried crying. I tried swimming. I prayed. I tried running. I tried sprint triathlons. I cried and I prayed. I tried Ironman distance triathlons. I tried pretending. I tried drinking. I tried hiding. I tried drinking more. I prayed. I wrote. I prayed. I wrote some more.

Following many steps in my recovery program, and a few years further on up the road, my thinking was that I should wait to write a book until my son was out of elementary school. I didn't want his friends to know about his dad in the ugly light the book might put on me. Then came middle school. Then high school, college, and law school. In the meantime, I continued to pray. I went to my recovery meetings. I went to outside abuse recovery groups. I stayed in recovery. I learned to trust and do the work necessary to heal. To let go. To forgive.

I even prayed that the thought of writing a book of my experiences to help others would just go away.

It didn't.

As you'll learn, I tried running one more time, but that nearly killed me.

And so here we are. At last.

This is my story, from the depths of despair and the gates of Hell, to redemption and gratitude. I'm loved. And I believe that. I choose love and I try to live that.

I forgive. Because I have been forgiven. I am again swimming, running (though my run is more of a walk-jog), and participating now and again in triathlons. Yes, my story may sound heartbreaking to some. To others, perhaps it can help them fight similar pains and demons, to seek help and believe in *hope for a better life.* May this offer a beacon of encouragement. Sorry it's taken so long.

*Fran Fidler*

CHAPTER ONE
# RUNNING

I often hear someone say I'm not a real runner.
We are all runners, some just run faster than others.
I never met a fake runner.

– Bart Yasso –

*"Stop!"*

I heard the cop yelling behind me, but I kept on running. If I could just make it to the beach, I was sure I could throw myself into the Gulf of Mexico and swim for it.

The cop must have wondered why I was so intent on getting away. What was I running from? What was I hiding?

It was two days before St. Patrick's Day, 1991. Earlier, I'd finished my shift as a waiter at a local breakfast and lunch cafe called First Watch, a block away from the Gulf of Mexico in Naples, Florida. My shift manager, John, had asked me if I would stick around after closing to do some prep work for the next day. "We'll get a few beers afterwards," he'd promised. Sounded good to me. I was thirty-five, living as if all was well and I'd be around forever.

When the time came, John suggested I run out and buy a six-pack, but I thought, *what's better than a six-pack?* and came back with a twelve-pack instead. We put on a homemade CD of Jimmy Buffet, started prepping for the next day, and talked and drank. John was a good guy, one of several friends I'd made since I'd moved to Florida from Boston four-and-a-half years earlier. I made friends easily. Drinking often helped.

With our prep work completed, we left the café in John's Jeep and had a couple more beers at a local hangout, and then John brought me back to the café's parking lot so I could get my bike, which I had ridden in on earlier that morning. It was right around 9:00 p.m. on a Friday night and neither of us was in a hurry. We were each still working on a beer as we sat in John's Jeep, headlights on, the only car in the small parking lot. This apparently looked suspicious to the cop who happened to be driving by, and he pulled in.

"Here," John said, handing me his beer can, "get rid of the beers. I'll talk to the cop."

I exited the passenger side and started walking, dropping the beers between the two buildings we were parked in front of. The thing is, I could have walked back to the Jeep and everything probably would have been okay. We weren't toasted, really. John was an amiable guy who would have merely explained to the cop that we were just finishing up work for the day. He was the shift manager at the restaurant; I was a waiter. Simple enough. "Have a nice night," the cop probably would have said.

But I didn't walk back. I started walking away.

"Sir," the cop said, raising his voice. "Come on over here."

I kept walking.

"Hey!" he repeated, a bit louder now. Then, in a commanding voice, "Come here."

*F--k it,* I thought. *I'm not going back.* Then I started walking faster until I walked right into the bike rack, flipping over it and landing hard. It happened so fast that it felt like I'd been shoved from behind.

The sensation panicked me and I got up and started running. I stumbled once or twice, a result of my adrenaline. I wasn't in great shape despite the fact that I'd been racing in triathlons for eight years. I had a nagging knee injury that had been pissing me off, keeping me from training the way I liked. Still, I felt that if I absolutely had to run, even two or three miles, I could do it. Of course, this was a different kind of running. I was running from a cop. I was running to escape. I was running for my life. And it was unfolding fast, so fast that I couldn't even take it in, couldn't grasp what was happening. All I knew was that I needed to get out of there. I needed to get away.

"Stop!" the cop yelled, chasing after me.

On the other side of Gulf Shore Boulevard, the main drag that ran along the beach, was a grassy park that separated the street from the white, sandy shoreline. I knew the park well from many an early 5:00 a.m. meeting with the local running group I belonged to. If I could just get through the park and then make it through the beach, I could hit the water. I'd be okay then. I could swim away and the cop would never catch me. I'd keep swimming, farther and farther out. The worst case scenario was that I'd drown, or maybe a shark would get me.

I stumbled a couple more times and the cop started gaining on me. My mind was racing but all at once, through the confusion and panic, three very clear thoughts came quickly into my head.

The cop could open fire on me. That was the first thought. He could shoot me in the back. *And that would be all right.*

The second thought was that I knew I had to deal with everything. I had to deal with my past, with my secret. That was now clear. I could run no longer from *it*. I could no longer keep *it* hidden. The running from the cop was as symbolic as it was real. It was senseless and irrational. But so was running from my past.

On the other hand, I could not expect that I'd be able to simply stop, turn around, face the cop, and reasonably explain this epiphany to him. This was my third thought. I was screwed. It was too late to say, "Sorry, Officer. I know now what I'm running from. Isn't that great?

Let's just call it my mistake. Sorry for the inconvenience."

And so I kept running. I could now hear the breaking waves of the Gulf. I was getting closer. But I stumbled one more time, which was just enough for the cop to catch me.

As clear as the three thoughts had been to me only moments before, once the officer tackled me and tried to keep me down, I kicked, clawed, scratched, and punched at him, screaming, "Get the f--k off me!" until I no longer had any energy to fight anything or anyone.

*I surrender.*

The officer had called for backup during the chase, and soon another cop showed up. And before long, I was in handcuffs.

Later, as the fog of the incident began to lift, I thought of the pure irrationality of my actions. Even if I had gotten away, by running or by swimming, how long would it have taken for the officer to have ascertained from John my name, my address, what time I was due to show up at work again? Five minutes?

The running was nonsensical, except within the context of *it*. And it had nearly killed me. But I knew it hadn't just been tonight. It had been my whole life.

But now I was done running. And the real journey was just beginning.

# CHAPTER TWO

# THE CELLAR

I inhale loneliness like it is the sweet smell
of virgin earth conquered by fiery rain drops.
Within me, I'm a thousand others.

– Faraaz Kazi, Truly, Madly, Deeply –

In 1993, a couple of years after my arrest, I entered the Boston Marathon. My knee injury was better and I was running well again. Just three months earlier, I'd run a marathon in Tallahassee, finishing in under three hours. Now, in Boston, I was off to a decent start. Running along Union Street, I passed the "Entering Ashland" sign. The course then veered onto Waverly Street and, three miles later, I passed the "Entering Framingham" sign.

Nevertheless, from the beginning of the race, I felt somehow...off. It was a strange feeling that I'd never really felt running before. Going into the race, I had had such great expectations. But at about nine-and-a-half miles, I had to stop running and start walking. *What the hell's going on?* I thought. I dug deep, telling myself to hang in there, to keep going. I was approaching two years of sobriety and thought I should be *flying*. Instead, I had hit a wall.

Then I looked up and saw the sign. "Entering Natick."

*Are you f--king kidding me?* Now I wondered if I even stood a chance of finishing the race. Natick? In previous races, I swore under my breath when I saw the Natick sign and put my head down and barreled past it. This year, it smacked me in the face, as if to say, "I own you."

I didn't finish the Boston Marathon that year.

Natick. It was the town where I'd spent much of the first four years of my life. A place where my memories were hazy, but the effects were still being felt. It was in Natick where much of the foundation of my childhood had been laid, a childhood that would only get worse from there.

My parents were married in February of 1952. My sister, Kathy, would be born in November of that year, and I would come along three-and-a-half years later. I was a very small baby—"tiny," my grandmother had observed, and that became my nickname from that time on. I was Tiny Fidler. I presume my parents divorced shortly after my birth. My first memory of my mother isn't until I was five, and I wouldn't meet my father until I was a grown man.

A lot of my childhood remains vague. Some of it I'm sure I've blocked out, which I'm learning to accept although it still kind of pisses me off. The rest, the bits and pieces that could conceivably be filled in by the memories of family members, remains missing due primarily to a disturbing code of silence or convenient memory loss. It seems to be understood that, though we may gossip about other people, we just don't talk about unpleasant things within the family.

I have exactly two memories of Natick. The first is of crying and peeing in my pajamas while waiting to use a bathroom. The second memory is of being outside in the rain, alone, handcuffed to a downspout, crying for my mother and having nobody come. This second memory came through a hypnosis session early in my recovery. There's no one to validate it, but there seems no question that Natick was not a healthy experience. Kathy tells me our foster father was the police captain of Natick (perhaps that explains the handcuffs) and that our foster mother killed herself in her kitchen in view of several foster children, including Kathy. Maybe it was this incident that finally sent us back to our mother.

Why we were in foster care in the first place remains a mystery to me. I assume our mother could not handle the job of raising us. Nevertheless, by the time I was four, Kathy and I were back with our mother in South Boston. Southie, as everyone referred to it.

Our mother lived with our grandparents on O'Callaghan Way in the projects. Kathy recalls that our mother was, for a time, a call girl working out of a penthouse apartment on Park Street in downtown Boston. I have no recollection of that in particular but later on, when we lived with her, I remember strange men coming and going.

Ma was the eldest of six. Our house was a single-family, two-story unit with a cellar, part of a row-house complex with a paved courtyard and a large backyard. There were train tracks beyond that. Upstairs, there were two bedrooms, one for my grandparents and the other for their three daughters—Ma and aunts Helen and Peggy—and Kathy. The cellar housed my grandparents' three sons—my uncles Joe and Larry and Frankie—and me. I remember only two beds downstairs for the four of us. Kathy tells me that Frankie slept with our grandparents until he was almost twelve. This would have been about the time we moved in.

In addition to the ten of us, relatives, friends, and the occasional parish priest often seemed to be popping in and there was always a lot of socializing and laughter. My grandfather had a piano in the living room, which he always played on special occasions—Christmas, Thanksgiving, St. Patrick's Day. Grandpa was kind. A gentleman, quiet but funny. He worked for the Boston transit authority and, as a young boy, I remember going with him to the Dudley T-station to watch him get the buses off on time. I loved my grandparents very much.

As for my mother, the positive memories I have of her mostly seem to involve the beach. A short walk from our house, through the projects, was Columbia Park, with ball fields and a mile-and-a-quarter-long sidewalk around the perimeter. On the other side of the park was Carson Beach, on the harbor shoreline. Our mother would sometimes take us there. At other times, we'd go to Frog Pond downtown or Tenean Beach in Dorchester, the next town over.

That first recollection I have of my mother, when I was five, is of her taking me to the Boys Club. You had to be six to belong. Ma told the person working at the desk that I was indeed six and quickly shushed me when I began to tug on her arm to object.

In addition to being close with my maternal grandparents, I was also close to my paternal grandparents, especially my paternal grandmother, "Nana." This, even though I'd never met my father. He had lived in the projects, too, on Logan Way, a five-minute walk away. I assume the proximity is how my parents met, but by the time we had moved back in with our mother from our foster home, our father, who'd gone into the army, had remarried and moved to Vancouver. His mother still lived on Logan Way and I would see her in church and drop by her house from time to time as I got older.

Eventually, Ma got a place of her own and took us with her. She'd gotten a waitressing job at a Howard Johnson's by the expressway. We didn't go far, staying in the South Boston Old Harbor Village projects and moving to a Rawson Street house at the end of a cul-de-sac not far from the Howard Johnson's. This is where I would often see the strange men coming and going, and so apparently Ma hadn't given up her other profession. At the end of Rawson Street and across Dorchester Avenue was the Southeast Expressway with the Howard Johnson's just off the exit ramp. In the other direction was a pedestrian bridge running above the expressway that would take us over to the Old Harbor projects, where my grandparents lived. It was maybe a fifteen-minute walk back to their place, and I went there often.

Ma would sometimes start drinking in the early evening, and before long it became a regular occurrence for her to throw either Kathy or me out of the house for laughing a little too loud about nothing, or making funny faces at one another, or maybe just running around the house. If she kicked Kathy out, I'd cry and beg to have Kathy allowed back in. If she kicked me out, Kathy would cry and beg to have me allowed back in. Kathy was a "wh--re" and I was a "worthless little s--t" or we were both "no-good f--king maggots." For her part, Kathy doesn't ever remember Ma calling her by her given name.

I would run frequently to the Boys Club or to my grandparents' house. I have a sense that early on my grandmother must have had a stern talk with my mother, admonishing her for her abusive behavior towards us, but she was apparently unable to get through to her and I imagine she eventually gave up. But my grandmother's door and her heart were open to Kathy and me, and she always gave us refuge—along with love, hope, nourishment, and clean clothes.

Still, I hesitated to spend the night there. Spending the night meant being downstairs in the cellar, which had its own risks. Risks that were much more menacing than even my mother's verbal or physical abuse.

One terrible memory of life on Rawson Street is of having a rat run up my pajama leg after dinner one night as I stood at the sink washing the dishes. Such was the condition of the house that a rat might suddenly appear from out of nowhere, but this one threw me into a state of hysteria. I screamed and cried. My mother was there. I don't remember her saying anything at all to me. If she did, it was probably to tell me to shut up. "Stop your crying or I'll give you something to cry about!"

Once, I opened Ma's purse to find it full of dollar bills. I assumed for years that she must have won big at the track or playing the numbers, but now it seems just as likely that she may have turned a trick for that money. Either way, I went out into the street and stood in the cul-de-sac tossing the bills up in the air and screaming, "We're rich! We're rich!" Ma heard the commotion and stormed out and grabbed as many of the bills off the ground as she could. Then she grabbed me and yanked me back inside where I took a beating. Shortly afterward, a little neighborhood girl who'd witnessed the whole thing knocked on the door with a fistful of the bills. "Here, Mrs. Fidler," she said, "I found these on the ground, too."

After dinner one night on Rawson Street, I was playing outside with friends and a piece of glass must have cut through my white sneaker, which then turned red from the blood. I didn't notice it until one of my friends pointed it out. "What happened to your foot?" he said. Looking back, I wonder if even then I was somehow becoming inured to pain. Or maybe I was just learning not to show it.

One memory that especially sticks with me is of the girl upstairs. She and her older sister would often babysit Kathy and me. This girl was probably twelve. I could not have been more than seven or eight, but we played doctor and nurse and our playing would become very real. One time, we ended up in a bed together, though I can't swear to exactly what happened. Another time we were caught together under a bed by Kathy and the girl's sister. I was too young to understand what we were doing, but whatever it was, I willingly went along with it. This presents an obvious but significant question: how can a child be sexualized at such a young age?

The answer goes back to O'Callaghan Way. Back to that cellar. Back to one particular night.

Frankie shared a bed with me when Kathy and I moved into that house when I was four. Maybe he'd been sleeping in his parents' bed up until that time, as Kathy remembers, but somewhere along the line, he must have been moved downstairs into the cellar with his two brothers and me.

Even at four, I knew it was wrong. In the middle of the night, I awoke to feel Frankie's hand go over my mouth. "Shhh," he said. At the same time, I felt his other hand go down my pajama pants. I froze. I was terrified of what he was doing and I began to weep. I didn't understand exactly what was happening, of course. But I knew it had to be wrong. It had to be very, very wrong.

# CHAPTER THREE
# STUTTERING

As commissioner, you're supposed to be objective.
It wasn't much of a secret, though, that I loved Fenway Park,
especially how it made you a participant.

– Bowie Kuhn, Major League Baseball commissioner –

I can't draw a straight line from the abuse—both my mother's brand of abuse and Frankie's brand of abuse—to the stuttering, but it doesn't take a trained psychologist to conclude that there was most likely a connection. By first grade, the stuttering had become bad enough that it was decided I needed to repeat the year. The funny thing is, that's how I found out I stuttered. I didn't realize it until then. On the last day of first grade, with me present, my mother and the school principal talked and I heard the principal say, "If we hold him back, I think he'll outgrow it." Outgrow what? I wondered. *What's wrong with me?*

I begged to be moved along to the second grade with my buddies. "What did I do wrong?" I cried. "I won't do whatever it is you say I'm doing anymore! I promise!" That's when I was told I had a speech impediment that until then I hadn't even noticed. Of course, as a kid, you very quickly become self-conscious about something like that, which only makes it worse.

It was hard out in the hallway at school seeing my friends walking into the second-grade classrooms while I was walking into my first-grade room for the second year. I was as smart as they were. I just had a speech impediment, which I didn't even understand. Rightly or wrongly, the unconscious message I gathered was that even if I was smart enough, I was going nowhere.

Once I discovered my stuttering and picked up on the discomfort and annoyance it caused in others, I avoided situations that required speaking in front of groups. Throughout my years of school, I would always be sure to miss the first day of every year. The first day was when the teacher would invariably go around the room and ask everybody to stand and introduce themselves to the rest of the class. What I once gave no thought to, I now couldn't face. *I won't do it,* I told myself.

I was held back in third grade as well, but it was for different reasons. By then, I was missing a lot of school days, and not just the first one of the year. Kathy and I frequently played hooky together. She skipped school less as she got older, but I kept skipping. Regularly, I'd sneak on the subway at Andrew Square, then take the trolley, joyriding out to Mattapan Square or Harvard Square and walk around. I loved the Coop, a bookstore serving both Harvard and MIT, with all its music albums and rock and movie posters. More often, I would take the train to Park Street, then take the trolley to Kenmore Square and go to Fenway Park to watch the Red Sox. A bleacher ticket was fifty cents and, once in the bleachers, I'd sneak through the grandstands, past the dugout, and around home plate to left field to watch "Yaz"—the great Carl Yastrzemski—up close. Eventually, I'd make my way back around to right field to see Tony Conigliaro, a local kid who'd made it to the big time. I'd hang around the bullpen, too, trying to get autographs, although I never got any. Often times, I couldn't get the words out to properly ask.

I'd always listen to Red Sox games on the radio, hearing the voices of Curt Gowdy and later Ken Coleman and Ned Martin. I knew the names of all the players. Billy Herman was the manager, and besides Yaz and Tony C., the Sox had Dave Morehead, Jim Lonborg, Earl Wilson, Frank Malzone, Bob Tillman, Felix Mantilla, Jim "Goo Goo" Gosger, Dick "The Monster" Radatz, and another local product named Bill Monbouquette. This was all before 1967—what would become known as the "Impossible Dream" season when the Sox won the American League Pennant on the very last day of the season. It was the first winning season for the Sox since 1958, and it solidified my love for the team. Later, when I was seventeen and eighteen, I'd actually work at Fenway as a vendor. I loved vending, but I probably did more game-watching than selling.

Besides skipping school in favor of Red Sox games, I'd often ride the subway into downtown. I'd walk along Washington Street, between Boylston and Kneeland in what used to be called the Combat Zone. There were strip clubs there and peep shows and hookers. Drug dealers, too. Not a place for a kid to be wandering around and, in truth, it always scared me a little to be there, but it was also exciting. There were a couple of music stores and old bookstores there, too, and I loved getting lost in the search for Red Sox and old Boston memorabilia, or any kind of Beatles collectible. It was like an archaeological dig. Nobody ever bothered me in the Combat Zone. Not even the cops. Never once did I get approached by a police officer asking me what I was doing there or why I wasn't in school or, if it was later in the day or evening, why I wasn't at home.

Kathy would write my notes, telling the teacher I'd been sick or something and then signing them with Mom's name. But then one time she refused. "I'm not writing any more notes for you," she told me. "It's not right. You should be going to school." I went in the next day with a forged note I'd penned myself. In front of the whole class, my third-grade teacher asked me who wrote the note.

"My mom," I answered.

"I'll ask again, Francis. Who wrote this note?"

Third grade or not, I had taken a lot of time with the note and it looked to me as real as anything Kathy had done. There was no way Mrs. Donovan could know it was forged. I stuck to my guns. Catching my breath, tapping my foot so I wouldn't stutter, I insisted, "My mother wrote the note."

"Well then maybe we'll just call your mother and see if she remembers writing it," she said.

A bluff. I was certain of it.

"Sure, go ahead," I shrugged. "She'll tell you." Even if it wasn't a bluff, I knew Mrs. Donovan wouldn't be able to reach my mother. She'd either be drinking or sleeping.

I was wrong on both counts; it wasn't a bluff and my mother took the call. She managed to make it into the school the following morning, where she and I met with Mrs. Donovan and the principal. The principal showed my mother the note and then Mrs. Donovan asked me once again who wrote it. I tried to tug on my mother's arm to let her in on my subterfuge with the hope that she'd be willing to join the conspiracy. It would be us against the school. But my tug was met with a hard, open right hand across my face. The jig was up and I was on my own.

I took the requisite beating when we got home, but a few days later, at a moment when I knew my mother was in a reasonably good mood, I asked her how the teacher knew that the note had not been written by her. "Because my name is spelled *M-a-r-y*," she said. "Not *M-a-r-r-y*."

Then she slapped me on the back of the head and swore at me for being stupid. I probably thought she was right.

I didn't skip school as often after that, but I didn't stop entirely. Later that year, I'd play hooky with a buddy named Johnny. Johnny and I shoplifted some things—a rubber ball, I think, and some novelty fake money—out of a five-and-dime store. We fled the store and then scooted down a tight alleyway we knew that no adult could follow us into, and somehow I managed to get grease stains on the brand-new chinos my mother had just bought for me.

I tried to hide the stains when I got home, but, of course, Ma spotted them. Furious, she demanded to know how I'd happened to ruin my new pants. I blamed it on woodworking shop. My friend Georgie, a couple years older than me and in junior high, had talked about woodworking shop, and it sounded plausible that one could get one's pants stained in such a grimy environment. Now Ma's fury was directed at the school. With me pleading with her that I could clean the grease off the pants and trying to assure her it was no big deal, she called the principal and tore into him, screaming at him for several minutes before the principal could finally interrupt and say, "But, Mrs. Fidler, we don't have a woodworking shop in this school."

Ma hung up the phone. "Tiny! Come here!"

I stepped nervously towards my fuming mother. She said nothing. Then she repeatedly slapped my head, face, and back. Finally, she seethed, "Get to bed! No dinner for you tonight!"

As soon as my mother had called the principal, I knew a beating would be coming. This was rare, though. Most of the beatings came out of nowhere with no real rhyme or reason. The beatings were scarier, of course, when you knew they were coming because then you had more time to think about them. And then there were the desperate debates you'd have with yourself: *Should I run away? Where won't she find me?*

As it happens, my friend Georgie was the son of the man my mother was soon to marry. Ma met Jack after we had moved from Rawson Street to the D Street projects. I don't know why we moved, but I know that D Street felt like a definite move backward. Although closer to the Boys Club, which I liked, the D Street projects were considered the worst in Boston. Compared to the other places we'd lived, D Street was a lot dirtier and more run-down. There was more fighting and crime, too. And more rats.

Jack was a strong, athletic guy; in fact, he'd played semi-pro baseball. He was an ex-Marine who worked for Boston Edison. His first wife, Joan, who had come over from Ireland, died, leaving him to raise five kids. Besides Georgie, there was Florence, Jackie, Danny, and

Michael. Though Georgie was older than me, we became good friends quickly after my mother and Jack started dating. Like his dad, he was an especially good ball player. Jackie was my age, and we became good friends, too, even going off to summer camp together in 1966 for a couple of weeks. When we returned, we were brothers. Ma and Jack had married while we were away.

Not long after that, we all moved out of the D Street projects to Knowlton Street, into a triple-decker across the street from the Old Colony projects. The first floor housed a bar, called Scat's Tavern, and a barbershop. The second floor was where the landlord lived. We lived on the third floor, where we made four bedrooms out of the apartment, one for Jack and Ma, one for Florence and Kathy, one for Danny and Michael, and one for Georgie, Jackie, and me. There was one bathroom.

The apartment had hardwood floors throughout that let us boys slide around in our socks when we could, which was pretty much when Jack was out and Ma was sleeping. We'd often play baseball in the living room, rolling up a pair of socks to use as a ball and using a hand as the bat. We were always creating bottom-of-the-ninth heroic scenarios, but the fun would end with the occasional broken lamp or knick-knack. Then came beatings and verbal abuse, being sent to our rooms for the day, and often being sent to bed without dinner.

The triple-decker also had a common roof deck with a great view of the city, where I would go up to hide, cry, or pray. Sometimes, I might just go up to take in the beauty of the city. And sometimes as a young teenager, I'd pretend I was one of the Beatles jamming to "Get Back" like they famously did on the rooftop of 3 Seville Row in London.

I liked my new stepfather. I was starting to get more into sports and I admired his athleticism. He could be funny, too. Quick with a one-liner, occasionally a crude one, which we kids always appreciated. But Jack drank. And he could be a mean drunk.

The drinking would typically start before Jack got home. By the time he'd arrive for dinner, we knew to be on our best behavior, tiptoeing around and being careful not to say anything too loudly. Sometimes even a word uttered under your breath could be picked up from the next room, and that would never end well. We never knew if any given night was going to be one of those nights when Jack was feeling more than ready to beat somebody for something. Anything. As with my mother, the beatings were mostly random or for insignificant infractions, like if you got home late, if you didn't finish your dinner, if your pajamas weren't on by a certain time, or if you just looked at Jack funny. Or if any one of us had given Ma a difficult time during the day, which might be defined as asking for an extra piece of cheese or putting too much peanut butter on a sandwich. The beatings would typically come by way of Jack's belt. Of course, Ma would often start cocktailing well before dinner time, which only made things worse.

We kids became close and we tried to look out for one another. But coming to a sibling's defense, as we all discovered the hard way, meant you'd be in for a beating, too, and so most of the times you'd just turn away, hearing the screams and the pleading, wishing you had the courage to do something but knowing you wouldn't. We talked about it as adults many years later. There's a trace of guilt I suppose we all feel for not doing more to stop the beatings. On the other hand, we were just kids. They were the parents, the ones whose job it was to protect us.

Kathy eventually left, although I don't remember exactly when. It seems to me she just sort of started spending less and less time at home, until eventually she just wasn't there anymore. I tried to get out of the house, too, with swim practice after school. On weekends, I'd make the ten-minute walk to O'Callaghan Way to my grandparents' house or stay with friends. By then, I had friends from O'Callaghan Way, friends at school, friends from summer camp, friends at the Boys Club (where I was spending more and more time), and friends around Knowlton Street, all separate groups of boys and girls who mostly knew one another by name but didn't hang around with each other. It would always be that way for me; I always made friends across a broad range of people and places. Ma used to say that I got more phone calls than anybody in the house. Danny saw my popularity and told me one time, "When I get older, I want to be just like you." I remember thinking, *oh, no, you don't.*

Looking back, I wonder if what I was doing was somehow trying to cover all my bases, making sure I had in place a support network of sorts. On some level, I think I even knew this at the time. Was making friends a way in which to further the fiction in my mind that nothing was wrong, that my life was normal? Was it a way to whitewash?

Even with all my friends, it was tough some nights finding a safe harbor when Ma and Jack were drinking. It seemed that everybody's parents drank. "You can't stay here tonight," a buddy might say. "My dad's drinking again, too." There were times when I would just stay out all night.

I found a safe haven in sports. I loved baseball—the sights, the sounds, the smells (the leather scent of a new Rawlings glove or the smell of the gum inside a pack of baseball cards). The unmistakable crack of the bat, a slide into second base creating a cloud of dust and the umpire yelling safe or out. I loved the infield chatter, encouraging the pitcher or heckling the batter. "Come on, fire it in there, fire it in there! Hey, batt-uh, batt-uh! Easy out, easy out! No batt-uh, no batt-uh! Swiiinng batt-uh!"

Georgie, Jackie, and Danny played organized ball. For me, it was mostly pick-up games. My friends and I would often play stickball over in Sterling Square and halfball in the street in front of our house on Knowlton. That's when the guys who frequented Scat's weren't playing halfball there. Halfball was a close cousin of stickball, where you'd cut a rubber ball in half. Half a rubber ball doesn't go nearly as far as a whole rubber ball when it's hit with a broomstick, and it's much less likely to break a window. The ball of choice was the pimple ball. Pimple balls were made of thin white rubber, and, as the name implies, they were pimpled. They were easier to cut in half and you could pitch with them better.

The batter's box was across the street—a grate that ran over a maintenance tunnel running between the brick project buildings. If you hit the halfball to the first floor of our triple-decker from there, you had a single. Second floor, a double. If you hit it up to our third-floor apartment, you had a triple. On or over the roof was a home run. Two strikes were all that was necessary for a strikeout, and a ball caught on the fly or off the building, a light post, a passing car, or anything else before hitting the ground was an out as well.

These are wonderful memories. Warm summer days or evenings playing halfball in the street, listening to music from someone's Zenith AM-FM transistor radio with "Woo Woo" Ginsburg on 1510 WMEX. The sounds of "Summer Wind" by Frank Sinatra or "Beyond the Sea" by Bobby Darin. The music of Motown, the Beatles, Blood Sweat & Tears. Laughter, joking, friendships, camaraderie.

I took athletics seriously, especially at the Boys Club. In a roundabout way, one of the things I found most helpful about becoming good in sports was that sports could do my talking for me. If I didn't get picked early for a team for some casual game of something because maybe nobody knew me, I'd make sure through my play that they'd remember me and I'd get picked early the next time. And it didn't require a speech or even an introduction. During play, I very rarely stuttered at all. I could shout, "I'm open!" or call a play or yell a profanity at somebody without a single hitch. Hell, I could yell a string of profanities and it would come out flawlessly.

And, of course, sports got me out of the house. So did the camps. When I was twelve, I went to work at Duxbury Stockade, about a forty-minute drive south of Boston towards Cape Cod. Duxbury Stockade was adjacent to Camp Wing, and they held winter camps during Christmas break. The following summer, I went to work at Camp Mitton in Brewster on the Cape, and I'd go back every summer and work there until I was seventeen. All the camps were affiliated with the Boys Club. My friend John "Goody" Goodwin was a two-miler on the track team, and at camp he'd run while I rode a bike alongside him. Then I'd swim the lake while he rowed a boat alongside me. I worked in the kitchen and the mess hall at Camp Mitton, eventually becoming a third cook. I got paid at Camp Mitton. Not much, but enough to give me some spending money when we'd go into Hyannis on weekend nights to play putt-putt golf, eat salt water taffy, and stand outside and listen to the music coming from inside the bars.

These were innocent times. Safe times. Back at the camp, I'd sleep soundly, in a way I could never sleep on Knowlton Street, and certainly not in the cellar of O'Callaghan Way.

By the time I reached high school, Jack and my mother had divorced. He'd gotten another woman pregnant and they'd moved to Dorchester, which was okay by me. But by then, Georgie, Florence, Jackie, and Michael had left too. Danny stayed, for which I will forever be grateful.

I heard that, eventually, Jack got sober, a goal that started back on Knowlton Street. One night, he had asked me to go with him to an Alcoholics Anonymous meeting. I never knew why—maybe because he didn't want to go alone. I remember the smoke-filled room in the basement of St. Augustine's Church. Jack was well-liked there, it seemed to me, and I almost felt a little like a celebrity being with him. Although I never saw Jack sober, I heard that when he died, he died with at least twenty-five years of sobriety.

# CHAPTER FOUR
# **SILENCE**

It's an all-encompassing feeling of helplessness,
staring into blackness and feeling completely
unable to pull yourself out of it.

– RACHEL HOSIE –

It would always start after I'd fallen asleep. One hand would go over my mouth, the other would go down my underpants. "Shhh," Frankie would say into my ear. As far as I remember, it only ever happened in the cellar at O'Callaghan Way, and only when my other uncles weren't around. But Frankie was a serial molester and an equal opportunity one, too. His sexual abuse extended to Kathy, who remembers being abused on Rawson Street during visits that Frankie would make. Maybe I was abused there, too, and I've blocked the memories.

I could never anticipate when it would happen. It would occur maybe six or eight times a year, it seems to me, but the number might have been higher. As much as I tried to remain aware, as much as I tried to stay awake and fall asleep late, I would inevitably let my guard down. Maybe I hoped that it had stopped, even convinced myself that it had. Maybe it was denial. Or maybe I was just tired and not thinking at all. I'd be at my grandparents' place, enjoying the evening, feeling safe, feeling as if everything was fine. And then I'd go down to the cellar, crawl into bed drowsy, and fall asleep all too easily, imagining the world was okay. Then I'd be shattered by the movement of Frankie's hand once again down the front of my underpants.

At that moment, I'd freeze, remaining as still as I could. I'd weep, silently begging God for help in a way that couldn't be formally considered prayer, but, as a child, it was all I had. Sometimes, Frankie would move his penis to my mouth and I'd clench my mouth shut as firmly as I could. Sometimes, he'd make me touch him. When it was over, I'd wrap myself as tightly as I could in my blanket. I'd feel dirty. I'd feel shame.

The abuse would continue until I was sixteen.

I could not tell my grandmother. Frankie threatened to tell her that I had started it. That I had asked for it. That I had enjoyed it. "I'm older," he'd tell me, "so she'll believe me."

This is how a pedophile instills shame. And from this shame comes a power dynamic that is hopelessly difficult to overcome. The abuser makes use of the shame that he has created. When I was eleven, Frankie caught me downstairs in the cellar one day with one of his *Hustler* magazines. I was sure that nobody was in the house, but all of a sudden there he was at the foot of the steps. I wasn't doing anything that any adolescent male wouldn't be doing, but the discovery by Frankie played into the guilt and shame and he wielded it like a weapon, threatening to tell, extorting me. The price was another incident of sexual abuse at the hands of Frankie.

I wonder, had that been the first time that Frankie accosted me, if I would have resisted. But years of manipulation, of shame fostered and nurtured from the age of four, made that impossible at that moment. Frankie had all the power.

I lived with twelve years of sexual abuse. It was my secret. I absorbed the shame. I carried the guilt—both the guilt of the sexual acts and the guilt of not shouting out *help me!* While it was happening, I learned to detach. I had to find a way to live as much and as often as I wanted to die. I found I could put my mind elsewhere for periods of time. I was aware of what was physically going on, but my thoughts would leave my body until it was over. I'd go somewhere else.

The times it would happen at night in bed, which was most of the times, I would cry myself to sleep after it was over, after my mind would return from wherever I had been able to let it drift. For several days afterward, I might take three or four showers a day, trying in vain to rinse the dirt and ugliness away. I would be furious with myself for letting my guard down, for thinking nothing would happen or believing that I could take care of myself. But I'd be equally maddened by the fact that I had to choose to sleep in my grandmother's cellar rather than take the constant barrage of insults my mother would hurl at me or be present while another man was in the house, having noisy sex with my mother in the room next to mine.

Why didn't I ever say anything to anybody, even in the face of Frankie's threats? Even in the face of the power that Frankie possessed through the years of manipulation? I wonder sometimes if, on some level, I suspected that Frankie's abuse was already known by close family members. Sometimes—most of the times—the idea seems far-fetched to me. Other moments, I'm not so sure. Part of my uncertainty stems from the silence that permeates our family to this day. The f--king silence. Nobody ever says anything. Who can say what was known and by whom? But my instincts tell me there's a chance, perhaps a slim one, that somebody else knew what went on in that cellar. And if I had those same instincts as a child—and children can be remarkably perceptive—then that might provide another reason why I kept Frankie's abuse to myself. Why risk having Frankie make good with his threats if other family members already knew? They hadn't helped me yet, after all, so why would they suddenly start? And if my family wouldn't help, then where would I even go?

Meanwhile, the outside world looked in on what, by all accounts, appeared to be a perfectly normal family. Relatives, friends, priests, and neighbors continued to drop by. My grandfather would play the piano and we'd all sing along to "Peg O' My Heart," or "Hearts Win, You Lose."

I did it myself. I portrayed normalcy at all costs, believing that the portrayal would make it so. We did fun things as a family. During the daytime, I even did things with Frankie. He and I and my other uncles would play stickball and basketball. We'd laugh together. Remarkably, later, I would even encourage Frankie to try to get his GED.

Why? Why didn't I punch his lights out instead? It's a question that would haunt me for years afterward. I can't say for certain. I suspect part of me felt it would be nobler somehow to rise above it. Turn the other cheek. Love thy enemy. And so, I'd just pretend that everything was all right. Besides, confronting the problem might have seemed to be a sure path to just exacerbating it. It would shine a spotlight on something I preferred remain hidden, something I was hoping would simply go away. What if it broke the family up? Then I'd be the reason. If I beat up Frankie, people would want to know why and it would all come out. What would become of me? Would I be sent back to the foster home? Deep down, I believed—I hoped—that everything would turn out okay someday. It wouldn't matter in the long run. *It won't affect my life. I'll be better.* So I thought. So I hoped. How could I have known that it would eat away at me for years and years? Nineteen to be exact, when it almost cost me my life. And so, till that day, I kept my secret, and I kept my silence.

# CHAPTER FIVE
# REFUGE

I want them to believe in themselves.
I only have so much time with them, so I try to give
them some tools. We have to encourage them. They need us.
Whatever problems young people have, they're our fault.
They didn't come to this world doing the things they did.
It's our fault. We dropped the ball, so we have to look in
the mirror and say, 'what else can I do to help them?'

– DENZEL WASHINGTON, GIVING TO THE BOYS & GIRLS CLUB –

The Boys Club was my safe place. I'd go there Tuesday through Friday after school and spend all day there on Saturday. Sunday and Monday, the Boys Club was closed, or I'd have gone then, too. At the club, I played pool, ping-pong, basketball, baseball, shuffleboard, and Skee-Ball. There were pottery classes, cooking classes, and art classes. I even tried boxing, dropping the idea before too long, figuring I was being hit enough at home. And I didn't like the idea of beating somebody else up either. All of this was in addition to learning to swim, and then being a part of the swim team.

Many of the pleasures from the Boys Club came in the friendships and in hanging out with the other boys. My favorite hobby was flipping baseball cards. We'd lean ten cards against a wall. The first kid would fling a card towards the wall, and if he knocked a card over, he'd get to take another turn. Depending on the angle of the card, you could knock two or three over at a time. Once you missed, it was the next kid's turn. The person who knocked the last card down won, taking all the cards in the process. There was always a Mickey Mantle or Willie Mays or Hank Aaron or Roberto Clemente card that was up for grabs, and we played for keeps. When there was a Red Sox in the pile, I tried a little harder. The loss felt a little more painful, too.

To buy baseball cards, I saved my money. I had a paper route. Jackie and I would often sneak out at night to go shoe-shining, too. We'd go downtown or to the bars around Knowlton Street, up and down East Eighth Street, to shine shoes. Seemed there was a bar or liquor store on every corner. We charged thirty cents and the fee was by design. If they didn't have a nickel to go along with a quarter, they'd often just give you a dime or even another quarter and tell you to keep it. If my mother came across the money I'd made, she'd often take it. She'd take the baseball cards, too, and throw them out. I took to hiding both.

There were a lot of good kids at the club. I became close friends with several on the swim team, and close with some other guys, too, like Michael Faith, even though he once threw a rock at me that just missed my eye. There were other great guys I swam with too, like Kevin Connolly, Paul Chapin, Billy Mullen, John Hunter, Gerry Dwyer, John Manning, Tim Burke, and Michael Faith's brother Richie, to name a few.

There were some real characters, too. There was a diver on the swim team named Kevin Weeks who was quick tempered, sometimes tending towards violent. Later, Weeks would become associated with mobster Whitey Bulger. He became a friend and a confidant to Bulger, ultimately going to prison for racketeering and narcotics trafficking but getting a reduced sentence for cooperating. There were some tough guys around the club, but that was the nature of the neighborhood. That was Southie.

But with all there was to do at the Boys Club, I liked being in the pool the most. In the pool, I could keep my head buried in the water. I could scream or cry or be angry in the water and nobody could tell. I felt invisible. And if I was swimming, I didn't have to talk, which meant I didn't stutter. And from time to time, with practice and focus, I swam well.

I started swimming competitively when I was around nine. It started one day when Harold Myroff, the swim coach at the club, asked Jackie and me to race the width of the pool and back. Jackie won, getting congratulations from Harold. Harold was a good guy who went on to have a wonderful coaching career. He had a gentle demeanor, but he loved winning. Watching Jackie get congratulated burned me up inside. At first, I couldn't make sense of it. I had tried my best. I swam hard. I had assumed I would win and when I didn't I found myself feeling hollow. It was maybe just a ten- or fifteen-second race, but it was a pivotal moment for me. From that point on, I told myself that I would never just assume I could win. I was always going to work to the best of my ability, and, at some level, it occurred to me then that working hard and practicing were necessary to become good at something. Maybe my competitive fire had been there all along, but on that day, it became clear.

There were intramural swim meets at the club and, as I got a bit older, I participated in swim meets against other clubs and boarding schools. I had a little talent, but my competitiveness was what really propelled me. I swam the butterfly, backstroke, and freestyle, winning medals here and there. Ma was actually proud of me and even took the time to attend some of the meets at the club, even though you could tell she'd been drinking. But, of course, this led to unrealistic expectations of me winning every time. I would try to rise to the occasion but would often fall somewhere between second and fourth. One time, I returned home on the bus from an away meet at the Charlestown clubhouse. I hadn't won anything, but it was evening and I knew my mother would have been drinking. I was afraid to go home, but I had nowhere else to go, plus it was a school night. I couldn't face the thought of telling Ma I'd come home empty-handed. In her drunkenness, she would have chided me. "My son the worthless f--king maggot couldn't even win one medal," she'd have said. So, I told her I'd won five races, fulfilling those unrealistic expectations. On the way home, I'd been jumped and had the medals stolen, I told her. "F--king bas---ds," she seethed. "It's okay, Ma," I said. After a half-hour or so, her ranting ceased. By morning she'd forgotten even talking to me.

I got more support from my uncle Joe, who would rarely miss coming to see me at my swim meets, something he'd continue doing all through high school. He had always been supportive. In fact, my aunts and uncles often filled in the holes where my mother and father should have been. Having lost all my upper teeth and several bottom ones before I was thirteen, Uncle Joe took me to the dentist, taking off work to accommodate the appointments and driving me to and from Somerville for checkups. Later, he would help me learn to drive. Aunt Peggy helped me with my stuttering. We'd often sing together. We had Friday "skit night" at my grandparents' house, and I'd put on a pair of my grandfather's trousers and Peggy and I would sometimes sing with Barbra Streisand's song "Sam, You Made the Pants Too Long" playing in the background. My Uncle Larry and Aunt Helen would jog together and invite me along for the mile-and-a-quarter run around Columbus Park, a long distance for me then. When Uncle Larry became a motorcycle cop, he'd sometimes put me on the back of his bike and we'd ride behind my grandparents' house. Helen would be the one I would often talk to when I had a problem.

On the street, there was still stickball and halfball with my friends. We played a lot of hockey, too. Street hockey, mostly. My junior high had an intramural street hockey league, in fact. My team had my close friends Michael Henry, Michael Faith, and Frank Vardaro, along with classmates and friends Stephen Harris, Andy Celiez, and Bob Dellasio. We lost in the finals 4-3. I was named MVP, but it was no consolation.

28

I walked home with my grandmother after that game and I cried all the way back to O'Callaghan Way.

We played ice hockey when Columbus Park would freeze over in winter. A neighbor near my grandparents' place would organize a caravan and take several of us out to Brookline to Larz Anderson Park, where we'd skate and play hockey on the pond. Sometimes, we'd go to Frog Pond in the middle of Boston Common, but you needed to get there early before the recreational skaters arrived. I fell a lot, but I played competitively.

It's the way I approached all the sports I participated in ever since that swim race against Jackie. On one Fourth of July, a bunch of us ran a race around the neighborhood backcourts and I finished first, and the mother of the boy who came in second came up to me and said, "You're going to the Olympics one day, I just know it." Unrealistic or not, the idea stuck with me and I often fantasized about being an Olympian.

Swimming remained my strongest sport, and if I was ever going to become an Olympic athlete that would be the path. For the time being, I just worked on getting better, swimming on the junior high school team and being named Most Valuable Swimmer in ninth grade. Meets were held at the Boys Club as neither the junior high nor the high school had their own pool. Then it was on to the high school team.

South Boston High School had been around since 1901. Seemingly everyone who lived in Southie had gone there. Ma had gone there. My aunts and uncles had gone there. My cousins had gone there. Uncle Joe had played on the 1956 South Boston basketball team, winners of the Tech Tournament—a tournament for all the local high schools in the region. That team was Southie's only championship team. It was still talked about in reverent tones and I started imagining how special it would be to win a championship for Southie High in swimming.

While I was enjoying my time on the high school swim team, some athletes from Boston College—basketball and rugby players, mostly—started coming around Southie. They'd been going into inner-city neighborhoods as part of a program to bring sports to at-risk kids, setting up Catholic Youth Organization basketball and flag football leagues. Of course, we didn't know we were "at-risk." Had they informed us of that, with a mixture of pride and ignorance and fear, we would have said "f--k you." But we didn't know and I joined the leagues and often made it a point to stick around after the games whenever I could. First, because I didn't really want to go home and, second, because I just liked being around these impressive athletes. Maybe I was hoping some of their athleticism would rub off on me. And they were good guys, too, trying to make something of their lives.

One time, after an Old Harbor Athletic Conference basketball game, with a few of us hanging around, the guys from BC said that if we wanted to, we were always welcome to come see them and they'd take us out to the BC sports complex. They'd get us in and we could take advantage of the facilities—the pool, the track, the tennis and basketball courts, everything. I don't know how I managed to get the words out, but I said, "Sure, I'll go!"

From then on, it became a regular thing for me. On weekends, if I wasn't swimming for the school or the club and my chores were done, I'd take the train and trolley to Chestnut Hill, sometimes alone, other times with a friend or two from the neighborhood or maybe a Boys Club swim teammate. One day, at the complex by myself after swimming laps in the college pool, the Boston College swim coach approached me. Tom Groden had started the swim program for the school just a year earlier. He would go on to coach the team for forty-five years, ultimately retiring in 2016. He asked me if I was going to try out for the team. "Well, I'm just a junior in high school," I said.

"Well, why don't we talk when you finish up here?" Tom said.

After I got out of the pool, we chatted and Tom invited me to have dinner that next week with him and his wife in their Chestnut Hill home. I was nervous, but I went. The dinner went well. I stuttered a bit, but all in all I managed to handle myself all right. Tom talked about how he was building a program and was looking for some quality swimmers.

I'm sure I must have told him I'd be interested in going to Boston College and competing on his team when the time came—mainly because I wanted to continue using the facilities. In truth, there were a few different reasons why I would not pursue the opportunity. Yes, it was BC—*Boston College!* But back at the club I had overheard a conversation one day, in which somebody had asked a part-time swim coach if I was a good swimmer. "Sure," he'd said. "I mean, good for around here. But if you were to send him to, say, Texas or Tennessee or some of the other places where the really great swimmers come from, it'd be a different ball game." I was still dreaming of the Olympics, and I was naïve enough, or ignorant enough, or just wanted to try *so badly,* that it occurred to me that if the great swimmers came from other places, then I needed to go to those other places.

A second reason was one I didn't arrive at on a conscious level. I could not have communicated it at the time, even to myself, but somewhere deep down I knew that, wherever I was going, I needed to get out of Southie, away from my mother, away from Frankie. I could not go to school and commute from home. I had to be on a campus somewhere far away.

But maybe the biggest reason I would not pursue the opportunity at Boston College had to do with the very kindness that Tom Groden had shared with me. This, too, was a subconscious inclination. This was the start of a lifelong pattern of shying away from scrutiny, of keeping my distance. I was competitive. I worked hard and I wanted to win. I wanted success. But if success meant the spotlight or more communication, then I'd just as soon pass. Socially, I wanted to be liked, just like anybody. But if being liked meant getting close to people, if it meant being open and honest and transparent and vulnerable, I had to back away. I didn't have that to offer. Getting attention meant people getting to know me. The real me. The me I kept hidden. I didn't want to expose or hurt my family with the ugliness or be so ashamed by the secret I was hiding. I just wanted to be a good guy, a good competitor, a good friend. My secrets—my stuttering, my mother's alcoholism and abuse, and, above all, Frankie's abuse—had to remain secrets. The stuttering I often had little control over, but I assumed the other secrets would remain secrets forever.

Some of the family dysfunction—the drinking, the beatings, the uniform silence—I often denied to myself. On the surface, I thought my family was great, and I acted as if it were. Surely we were normal. Maybe I didn't want to think otherwise because thinking otherwise would force me to confront just how dysfunctional we were. It would have meant having to come to grips with the idea that our lives were in danger on any given day we went home. It would mean having to face the fact that there were beatings, that sometimes the refrigerator would be padlocked, that on a few occasions I'd come into the kitchen for breakfast to find someone passed out from the night before, somebody I might not even know. One time I came in and woke up a stranger who yelled at me, "What the f--k are you doing?" and I threw a bowl of cereal at him and ran out. Facing all of that meant I'd have to do something about it. I was crying enough trying to survive everyday. That took enough energy. Change? What would that take?

But my denial could only go so far. Every now and then, I'd get a social hint that how I was being raised was not exactly ideal. In junior high, I liked a girl, and we were talking one day and kidding around and I called her a maggot. Suddenly, the mood of the conversation changed. "That's not nice," she said. "That's not a nice thing to say to *anybody.*" I flushed crimson. It had slipped out, but it had slipped out easily. Referring to somebody as a maggot didn't imply consequences for me. I'd been called it so many times the insult had lost its meaning. Having somebody call me on it was a sobering realization that my normal didn't necessarily align with the rest of the neighborhood's normal.

For the most part, though, I could blend in well with the kids in and outside Southie. My mother's alcoholism? Hell, most everybody's parents drank. The beatings? Most of us took beatings. All my friends had problems at home; some we would talk about, some we knew about without talking, and some were never shared or even hinted at.

Of course I kept the Frankie stuff and most of my mother's abuse inside, but I was always willing to listen to a buddy share his troubles. And despite my insecurities and fears of people getting too close, I made a lot of good friends. Sports helped. So did our neighborhood "five-buck sucks," with guys all pitching in five dollars so we could buy as much beer as possible. I started drinking at fourteen at summer camp, which was actually somewhat late for the guys and girls I hung around with. We'd drink Schlitz, Miller, Budweiser, Colt 45, and anything else we could get our hands on, like Maximus Super, a malt beer that was nine-percent alcohol. Sometimes, we'd shotgun the beers— punching a hole in the bottom of the cans, pulling the pop tops, and chugging them down. The first time, I was sick as a dog and I loved it, at least the following day after I slowly came to. Sometimes, we'd do the five-buck suck and then all chip in a little more for an ounce of pot. We'd hang out and listen to music. Friends played guitars, and there was always some sweet harmonizing going on. Always there was the music. And always there was the laughter.

I did a lot of hitchhiking to Cape Cod and back, too, often going with Michael Faith and other friends like Johnny Leonard, Sean Martin, Frank Vardaro, Enzo Stuart, and Michael Henry. One hot Sunday afternoon, Faithy and I were hitchhiking home along a lengthy stretch where cars just kept passing us by. Afternoon showers came and went, and Michael and I started singing, our song of choice being Frankie Valli's "Can't Take My Eyes off of You," singing the chorus over and over, and progressively louder.

One late night, Johnny and I had been walking for quite a while on Route 124 near the Cape before somebody finally pulled over for us. I was ready to jump in the front seat when Johnny, leaning in to tell the driver where we were headed, suddenly yanked me out by the back of my shirt. "We're good," he told the driver. "We don't really need a ride." After the car took off, Johnny told me of the naked male magazines he'd spotted on the floor of the front seat, right at my feet as I'd been getting in. It was a scary thought for a moment, but then we were soon laughing about it. Still, it made us a little more aware from then on.

Hanging out with friends, the talk, like it does for most adolescent boys, often turned to sex. My buddies were advanced. I liked girls and had my first girlfriend when I was thirteen. Through high school, there were various girls I'd go with for short periods of time, but through my early years of high school, sex wasn't anything that I was secure enough to try. Nor could I imagine that it would appeal to the girls I dated. My sexual experience consisted of abuse from an uncle. Sex was shameful for the most part. One time, a friend of mine was giving me advice about a girl I was seeing, telling me how I should "feel her up" and other tidbits of adolescent counsel. I remember thinking, *s--t, I don't want to* lose *her! Why would I do any of* that?

As I approached my senior year of high school, I continued thinking about the idea of bringing Southie that city swimming championship. I was voted team captain by my teammates, and the possibilities excited me. But the 1974-75 school year at South Boston High School would be like no other, before or since.

In 1965, the Racial Imbalance Act had been passed by the Massachusetts General Court. The Act called for school desegregation. Any school whose student body was more than fifty percent minority was considered to be "racially imbalanced" and was required to desegregate or risk losing its state funding. This included the Boston School District, which for several years, disobeyed the Act until, finally, court action forced the district to comply. A busing plan was created by Judge W. Arthur Garrity. It was decided that the entire junior class of Southie would be bused out to Roxbury High, a predominantly black school, while the junior class of Roxbury would be bused into Southie. Half the sophomores from each school would also make the switch. The seniors could stay put.

The plan did not go over well.

On the first day of school, only 124 students showed up out of 1,300. A rare first day of school for me, I was one of the attendees. But parents and residents showed up en masse, hurling rocks and bricks at the buses that were bringing the Roxbury kids in. Police rolled up in riot gear, but not before several of the black kids got hurt. Things calmed a little over the course of the next few weeks, but the tension wasn't going away any time soon. It was palpable within the community, and it was palpable within the school itself. Racial incidents were common.

As for the senior class, we were just trying to have as normal a year as we could. We managed to hold a senior prom, and I went with Noreen Ford, a pretty, sweet and kind girl that I was dating at the time. As for swimming, my hopes for a championship were dashed, as several of our best swimmers were juniors and were either being bused to Roxbury or attending the private schools their parents decided to send them to. When we lost to Boston Latin, the hope to become city champions was officially snuffed out.

Through everything, my friends and I still hung out, and we tried as best we could to enjoy our final year of high school. One night in December, Michael Faith and I went to see George Harrison at Boston Garden. It was his first tour after the Beatles. The very next day at school, Michael was stabbed by a black student in the hallway between classes. Word got out, and by mid afternoon a mob of hundreds had gathered around the school to confront the black students, basically trapping them inside. Decoy buses were brought in, and the black kids were smuggled out a side entrance while cops tried to keep the crowd at bay, many in the crowd throwing cans and rocks. The school was forced to close for a month. When it opened, we had to enter through metal detectors, and hundreds of police officers guarded the hallways and grounds. Michael spent some time in intensive care but would make a complete recovery.

The year proceeded, and I just tried to make my way as best I could, finding refuge in the pool and in time spent with friends. That's where I sought normalcy, whatever the hell that was.

# CHAPTER SIX
# NO MORE

You will never know the power of yourself
until someone hurts you badly.

– UNKNOWN –

There were a handful of good times I had with my mother. She was an avid Bruins fan, and on a few occasions when I was in junior high and high school we went to Boston Garden together to see the Bruins play. This was back in the Bobby Orr days, and one of my favorite players was Terry O'Reilly. Earlier favorites were Teddy Green, Johnny McKenzie, and Derek Sanderson, all tough-as-nails players who didn't take any s--t from anybody. Ma really enjoyed herself at the games, getting into the spirit of the action, standing and cheering and repeatedly yelling, *"Hit 'em!"* Those times came around just enough to make me wonder about what might have been. They gave me a glimpse at the light—maybe even happy—side of my mother. It was always short-lived.

Ma was probably happiest during the first year or two of her marriage to Jack. I seem to recall fewer beatings from her (and from him) in those early days. But after the marriage went south, and especially after Jack left, Ma was miserable. Ma normally started drinking in the early afternoons, and it was every day. We talked very little. I'd come home from school and she might ask me how my day was or how swim practice was, but there was rarely a follow-up question unless I'd come home from a swim meet, and then it was, *"Did you win?"* Looking back, it strikes me that it was no wonder we could never communicate on larger things. We couldn't even talk about the small things.

The beatings continued and so did the verbal abuse. Both would frequently come out of nowhere and were typically before dinner time, but sometimes she'd actually wake me up at night for no reason but to slap or whack me and call me a no-good name and then say, "Now get to sleep." There were times when she could be especially cruel. One night when I was fifteen, Ma had friends over and they were all drinking. I went to bed, and sometime after I'd fallen asleep, Ma slid a live lobster into my bed. I had an irrational fear of lobsters at the time. The claws had always spooked me from the time I was little, and Ma thought it was funny. I woke up to a lobster in my bed and a lot of delirious laughter from Ma and her friends. They laughed even harder when I screamed in fright.

There were several times I tried to talk to my mother in the morning after another evening of her heavy drinking where she had hit me or screamed at me with all the usual profanities and epithets. "This has to stop, Ma," I would say. "The drinking has to stop." I know, she'd say. But acknowledging the problem was as far as she would ever get. Never would she apologize. And by the time the afternoon would roll around, any remorse was forgotten and the drinking would begin anew. I don't know; maybe she used the drinking to cover the remorse.

One day, when I was seventeen, I came home from school to change clothes and head for swim practice at the Boys Club. It was an early spring day, sunny and clear. Winter was over and the trees were budding and I felt cheerful. I trotted up the creaky steps to our apartment. Ma had been listening for me. I was barely in the door before she started hitting me, smacking me hard on the face and the back of my head, calling me a son of a b---ch and worse.

Maybe it was the interruption of a rare, pleasant spring day—the jarring difference from the outside world (which I always imagined as being beautiful and safe and hopeful, even if it wasn't a pleasant spring day) to the world in our apartment. Or maybe it was just the last straw. Maybe it was time. I don't really know. All I know is that in a split second I found myself with a hold of Ma's throat. I pinned her against the back of the front door and held her there.

*"No more!"* I screamed into her face. "You hear me?! This has got to stop! *No more! No more hitting me!"*

I was shaking and soon crying as the realization of what I was doing hit me. Then I released her and went into my room. I kept shaking. Eventually, I calmed down and escaped into some music, putting the Beatles' *Revolver* and *Rubber Soul* albums on my stereo and listening through the headphones, letting the songs blast away as I sang along. In time, I fell asleep on my bed. No swim practice that day. Dinner was especially quiet.

Nothing was ever said about the incident. Like everything else, the matter was met with silence. But I could feel something change. Ma wouldn't stop verbally berating me from time to time for no reason, but that was the last time she ever hit me.

What might have emboldened me that day was an incident that happened several months before. An incident with Frankie.

One Friday, I had stayed the night at my grandparents' house. Frankie hadn't tried anything that night. Saturday morning we all had breakfast. Then it was time for my grandparents to go to the Capital grocery store for their weekly shopping. This would leave just Frankie and me in the house.

I was standing at the divider of the living room and kitchen, the kitchen being towards the back of the house. Frankie was sitting on the couch in the living room. There was small talk about the day's plans and what chores needed to be done. I began feeling uneasy, but

I wasn't sure why. I felt Frankie's eyes on me, though, and I was hit with a strange *what's going on?* kind of a sense. Nonchalantly, I asked my grandparents if I could tag along with them. But there were those chores that needed doing. Soon, I felt my adrenaline rise, and I was overcome with feelings of dread and uncertainty.

Then my grandparents made for the front door with Frankie still looking at me. Frankie had never abused me during the day; it had always been in bed at night. But the look on his face was unmistakable. Something was not going to end well. In past incidents, I always tried to stay awake or believe I could wake up before Frankie tried anything, and I was always taken by surprise. Never had he tried to attack me with enough time for me to actually contemplate what was going to happen. Never had I had this much time to know on a visceral level that something *was* going to happen. The inevitability of it gave me a dire sense that I had to get out of the house. *Now.*

I watched the front door close as my grandparents left. Frankie immediately rose and went to lock the door behind them. I didn't stick around to find out what was going to happen. I knew. I ran out the back door as though I were running for my life. The screen door slammed behind me, and I heard Frankie repeatedly yelling, "Come here! Get in the house!"

"No!" I yelled back. "No way! No way am I coming in. You're done! *Never again!* It's over! *No more!*" And then I repeated it: *"No more!!"* It was a frightening moment, but it was also liberating. I was now taking charge. Finally, I was awake and could see this ugly person for what he was.

Two doors down the commotion brought Mrs. Powers to her back door.

"Tiny, is everything all right?" she said.

"It's okay, Mrs. Powers, but I'm not going back into that house until my grandparents get back."

In fact, I didn't even wait for that. I ran on out through the next court, going to a friend's house and hanging out with him for the rest of the day.

And that was it.

For the next fourteen years, I'd be safe from Frankie. The abuse stopped that day, just like my mother's physical, emotional, and psychological abuse would stop less than a year later. In neither case can I imagine that the strength, power, or courage to confront both of them came from within. Yes, I was getting older, and through sports and friends I had gained some confidence, but this was more than confidence. I was not that strong. I'd never been that strong. I had always prayed for help, without having any idea how that help might arrive, or if it would arrive at all. Suddenly, I was lent the strength that I knew I had not possessed. My prayers had been answered.

Now all that remained were the scars. But the scars ran deep. Deeper than I even knew at the time. Way deeper.

# CHAPTER SEVEN
# DUALITY

Heroes aren't supposed to do bad things.
That's what villains are for. So either the good supersedes the
bad, or the bad makes it impossible to remember the good.
We don't like it when such duality exists in one person.
We don't want to know our heroes are human.

– LZ GRANDERSON –

Frankie attempted to be friends with me after I'd told him no more. I guess he thought if he couldn't molest me, he was determined to at least make sure we were on civil terms so that I wouldn't talk. And as far as I was concerned, I thought I could bury this ugly secret and deal with the shame of it through hard work, prayers, and tears. How else to explain that, a year later, Frankie would ask me to be the best man at his wedding, and I would accept? He'd been dating a girl named Diane, and they had decided to marry. At first, I thought his request was a joke. But Frankie was serious. Had he asked Larry or Joe? Had they told him no? Had Gram put him up to it? I didn't know. Looking back, it seems more likely that he wanted to keep me close to him, to keep me quiet. And, of course, to portray once again the idea that we were a functional family. I wanted that, too. That's probably why I said yes. What if I'd said no? What kind of questions would I face if that got out?

I planned nothing to say at the reception, and when the DJ announced that it was time for the best man to make his toast, I panicked. I managed to stutter something about wishing the couple a long, prosperous life, and then I just acted goofy out of nerves and picked up a piece of lettuce and tomato out of my salad and placed them on Frankie's head, hoping for a laugh that would distract the guests from the fact that I didn't have anything of substance to say.

It was starting to become clear to me around that time that I needed to get away. After high school, I was given the gift of acceptance at Bridgewater State College, about a forty-minute drive south of Boston, where I could join the swim team. A couple of other swimmers from our Boy's Club team were going to Bridgewater and I visited the campus and met the dean and assistant dean of admissions and felt comfortable there. Bridgewater was just far enough away that I needed to live at the school rather than commute from home. It was a step towards getting away from Southie—getting away from Ma and Frankie.

You can take the boy out of the projects, but you can't always take the projects out of the boy. I didn't have a lot of the basics when I got to Bridgewater. I didn't even have a toothbrush. I borrowed my roommate's the first day when he was out of our dorm room and told him about it upon his return. Such was my level of unworldliness that it didn't occur to me that he might have a problem with that. He did, as it turned out. In fact, he was so grossed out that I bought him a new one and got a new roommate. Why I couldn't wait and find a campus store to just buy myself a new toothbrush, I still don't know. I guess I'd been sharing things for so long that it simply didn't occur to me. His toothbrush was just *there,* and I picked it up and used it.

I made friends with a bunch of guys at Bridgewater, both on the swim team and in the dorms. For fun, we'd play tennis, do a short run, meet at the Rathskeller for beers and music, or just hang out and talk late into the night. Meeting people from all over opened up my world. Sometimes Noreen would drive down and visit, and sometimes I would hitch a ride home from a friend or take the bus back to Southie. Noreen had stayed in Southie after high school, getting a job at a bank. We would start drifting apart, though, both of us meeting new people and just growing up. During the middle of my second semester of that first year, I would start dating other girls.

The swim season started in September, right at the beginning of the first semester, and once again my athletic ability helped me fit in. My work ethic and focus spoke for me. So did my performance, on occasion. I was able to verbalize encouragement to the other swimmers, too, and this helped me form some bonds with my teammates.

But even with the camaraderie on the swim team, and even with the socializing, I still felt apprehensive and insecure, and I kept my distance from people. I still wouldn't dare allow anybody to get close. I still had that secret inside—that ugliness that I couldn't let anyone get a glimpse of.

This inner conflict manifested itself as a duality of character. There was the guy that others saw and there was this other guy I felt deep inside of me, and they were two different people. For my part, I was continually stuck with the guy deep inside and I could never see what the others saw. I saw ugliness. I felt ugly. Not always, but often enough. I was good at keeping that ugliness from others, however, and I was just as good at keeping my feelings about that ugliness to myself, at least most of the time. Nobody could see what my secrets were doing to me. They might see a guy at the Rathskeller having a beer and a slice of pizza, sitting back and enjoying the music. What they wouldn't see was that that guy wasn't having *a* beer; he was having five or six. Years later, someone would astutely say to me, "You know, you're a real Jekyll and Hyde."

This duality, and my underlying anger, was just starting to grow and reveal itself in those days at Bridgewater. So was my awareness of it. I knew I needed somebody to talk to, somebody to confide in. Henry Fanning, the dean of admissions, had taken a liking to me, and I found him relatively easy to open up to. He didn't exactly have an open-door policy, but I always felt I could drop by his office and chat with him about anything that was going on with me. One day, I told him about Frankie. It was the first time I'd told anybody.

Fanning must have known my issues were more than he could help with, apart from just listening, and he recommended a counselor for me to see. I didn't feel as comfortable with the counselor. He seemed a bit smug, as though his degree somehow made him an expert. I didn't tell him about Frankie. Instead, I told him of the pressure I was feeling with respect to my swimming aspirations. It was true even if it wasn't the whole story. At that point, I didn't know what the whole story even was. I just knew how I felt about myself, and it wasn't very pretty, but I was sure that if I could become a top swimmer, even an Olympian, *then* everything would be all right in my world. I'd be admired and respected. I'd be loved. Nothing that happened up until then—not Ma's abuse nor Frankie's abuse—would matter any longer. My problems would all go away. And so I demanded better things of myself and created unrealistic expectations of being the best. In the meantime, the ugliness wasn't going away, and so it was always one step forward and two steps back.

If I talked with the counselor at all about the real root of my problems, I probably didn't come any closer than revealing Ma's drinking. I'd tell him that sometimes after visiting home and once again seeing Ma drinking so heavily, it was hard for me to get back into the routine of school and swimming. This meant putting even more pressure on myself to grow and change. I felt as if I should have been able to rise above Ma's drinking, that I should have had the strength to pull myself up by my own bootstraps and move on with life. In a total of five sessions, that's as much as he would get out of me. I would never talk about Ma's continual verbal abuse, which hadn't stopped, and I sure as hell would never talk about her earlier physical abuse. There I was, still keeping the family picture intact.

One time, there was an alumni meet coming up and I was especially excited about it. I worked hard. I focused. Sometimes I would wear a t-shirt in the pool during practice, and occasionally I would even swim wearing a sweatshirt, forcing me to work harder to get through the water. I was training to win. "What will happen if you don't?" asked the counselor at one of our sessions. Of course, he meant for me to literally consider the possibility. What *if* I didn't win? The world wasn't going to end was his point. But to a boy from Southie, the question was an insult. What the f--k do you mean, *"What if I don't win"?* There I was, trying to convey to the counselor that I was working hard towards winning and felt that I could do it and he just kept saying, "But what if you don't?" He might as well have been saying, "I think you're going to lose." *F--k you,* I wanted to say. *What do* you *know?* He was *my* counselor; he needed to be in my corner and see my vision. The question pissed me off, and my attitude, in turn, pissed the counselor off, too.

In fact, I did win in that alumni meet and, in my mind, found no reason to return to the counselor. Screw him, if he wasn't going to support me. Of course, he was right: winning was more important for me than it should have been. But because I'd withheld my secrets, he could not have known exactly why he was right. I was trying in the only way I knew how, at the time, to create a world in which to survive.

This idea of wanting to overcome the damage that had been done by Frankie—the shame and guilt I never stopped feeling—by simple success in some form or another would become a lifelong pursuit. Of course, at that time, I didn't have the awareness to see the futility. If I could be a successful swimmer, then I'd feel better about myself. If I could have a girlfriend who loved me, if I could just be a good person and friend, if I went to this school or that school, or moved here or moved there—then the horror in my head would subside. I couldn't see that I was on a hamster wheel.

And yet I did at least have the awareness to know I needed to talk to somebody about the sexual abuse. But one of the first things that gets victimized by sexual abuse, maybe abuse of any kind, is trust. I couldn't imagine anyone believing me. And even if they did, would anyone be sincere enough to help me and not hurt me? Besides, what kind of help was I looking for? Frankie to go to jail or me to go to a psych ward? No, I wasn't ready to trust. From my childhood and through my youth, I had close friends and family members. But there was a clear line. Although I would easily trust some of them with my life, I could never trust them with my secret.

During my first year at Bridgewater, I did okay in swimming but not so well in the classroom. I majored in physical education with elementary education as a backup. My grades were poor, but good enough to at least get me through the year.

I went back home over the summer where I met a lovely girl named Beth at a popular Southie nightspot called the Mad-Hatter. She was going into her senior year of high school. By this time, I was more comfortable dating. My earlier reluctance to be sexually assertive had given way a couple of years earlier at the hands of a hospital receptionist who was a couple years older than me. I had met her while being diagnosed with Wolff-Parkinson-White syndrome, a benign heart irregularity. Shortly before I'd started dating Noreen, we'd had a couple of dates, and I lost my virginity to her. She was the aggressor, of course. I hadn't been ready to take the lead, but after that night I realized sex didn't have to be shameful and unpleasant.

Anyway, Beth and I were together through the first semester of my second year at Bridgewater, where I was finding it more and more difficult to keep up academically. I began to struggle with my social life as well. I was seeing the same people in the same settings day after day. They were getting to know me, which I found unsettling. I often felt as though everything I was trying to hide was beginning to show through, like cracks in a glass, ever so small at first but gradually growing. Coupled with my academic struggles, and my being too embarrassed to ask for help, it added up to an overwhelming feeling of needing to just *move*. I went home to Southie.

Back home, I figured on taking some time to refresh, renew, maybe get some advice, and reassess what I wanted and where I was headed. Returning to school wasn't entirely out of the question, but I knew it would take a much greater commitment than what I had shown and what I thought I was capable of making. Ma said nothing at all about my grades. Gram was disappointed. She had tried to encourage me as best she could—just as she'd always done. Nobody had ever encouraged me like Gram. But toward the end of 1976, she'd lost the love of her life, my grandfather.

I missed Grandpa so much that I couldn't clearly see at the time how bad Gram was hurting, how much his death had taken out of her. My grandfather's death had hit me hard. He was a great man to me. I never saw him drunk, he always came right home after work, and I never heard a curse word from him. To this day, I think often about the times he took me with him to work as a starter for the Boston MTA. I think of the piano he played in that row house in the projects. I think about the card and coin tricks he'd perform. I remember summer weekends with him and my grandmother and aunts Helen and Mary. Cookouts in the front yard, splashing in the pool out back; friends, family, and visitors dropping by always unannounced, always welcome. We'd go to Lake Winnipesaukee for a week and rent cabins. Sometimes, we'd go to Canobie Lake or Sunset Lake or Weirs Beach. We'd have cookouts. I remember as a little kid going away for a week at a time with them, a full family vacation. In these memories, I can never seem to place my mother. I don't recall her being there with us.

In any event, I tried to explain to Gram that I really wasn't smart enough to stick it out at college, that maybe college wasn't for me. In truth, although it had been nice to get away, there were moments when I figured I was destined to stay in Southie all along. I figured I'd become a waiter or a bartender or a cook and get my own apartment. Sure, it would most likely be in the projects, but it would still be my own place. What more could I aspire to? My grandparents seemed to have done all right, after all. Who was I to think I could do better?

That summer, I met my father for the first time. I was twenty-one. My paternal grandparents were celebrating their fiftieth wedding anniversary and my father flew in from Vancouver where he'd been living. As far as I knew, it was his first time back, and he came with his wife and their two little boys. There were a lot of people who went to meet him at the airport, including several cousins on that side of the family. Kathy and I drove out to the airport, too, and Danny came along with us.

I was nervous, but also excited. I wanted to see the man who was my father, maybe even get to know him. Maybe we could have a relationship. At the airport, everybody formed an impromptu receiving line as my father and his family got off the plane. I took my place at the end of the line (of course) hoping that by the time my father got to me, my name would have already come up. I'd have been pointed out to him. This would save me from having to stammer through an introduction.

It didn't work. Eventually, my father made his way to me and asked, "Now, which one are you?"

"I'm *T-T*-Tiny," I said. "I'm *yor-yor*-your son." Immediately, my father excused himself to go to the bathroom, and I stood there watching him walk away. He hadn't even said so much as "nice to meet you."

Things got even more awkward when everyone was walking out of the airport and Kathy offered our father a ride in our car, which he accepted. Kathy and Danny were in the front seat, and it was my father and me in the backseat with nothing to say. Getting out of the parking garage, the car stalled. This provided a welcome reason to get out of the car. I popped out of my side and walked around the back of the car to give it a push, something my father also decided to do from his side *at the exact same time*. I thought afterward that if anyone had been watching, we must have looked like two f--king Mexican jumping beans popping out of the back doors. Now, instead of being seated next to each other in the back seat with nothing to say, we were standing next to each other behind the car with nothing to say.

We pushed and watched the car slowly roll down the parking lot ramp. Kathy was able to pop the clutch and start the car up, and then she drove a few hundred feet to get the engine turning, with me wondering where the hell she was going. My father and I were soon walking together to catch up to the car. It was ten o'clock on a clear summer night, and there was nobody else around. It was just us and the stars and the lights of the Boston skyline. Finally, I heard my father say, "So what's new?" *What's new?!* I thought. *This is what you have to say after twenty-one years?* There were a thousand and one thoughts racing through my head that I wished I could have shared with him at that moment, a hundred or more memories of times I wished he could have been there. I started a word, hoping I could make it into a sentence, but I knew it would end in me stuttering helplessly. "Nothing," I finally managed to stammer lightly in reply. And then we walked in silence to the car.

My father spent a few days in Southie. I saw him at the anniversary party, and he also joined some of my cousins and me at a pub one evening around the corner from Dorchester and Old Colony streets. It was crowded that night, and we sat at a long table and I listened to him talk of the army and of his self-proclaimed heroism in saving another soldier one time. I waited for him to ask something about Kathy and me. He never did. Then he went back to Vancouver.

I might have been back home in Southie during that summer, but my sense of who I really was wasn't becoming any better defined. The duality was ever present. I took bar-back and busser jobs at a couple of restaurants in Faneuil Hall, Boston's historic marketplace. One day, off from work, I was walking through the marketplace by Lilly's where I worked with some friends, and one of them had a camera. It was a pleasant summer day, and the corridors of the Hall were crowded with tourists and residents alike. I asked my friend to take a picture of me in the midst of the crowd. I didn't tell him why. I wanted to know if I could find myself in that crowd, if I would be able to tell which one was me. Later, he gave me the developed photograph and I spent a lot of time looking at it. I knew where I'd been standing, and I could see the person that was me, but somehow it still seemed like a stranger standing there looking back at the camera.

My stuttering wasn't getting any better, either. There were times I thought it was actually getting worse. I tried things on my own to cure it. Once I'd read about an ancient Greek orator named Demosthenes, who was said to have cured his stuttering by talking with pebbles in his mouth. I was willing to try anything, so I tried that. Demosthenes's treatment actually helped a little in the beginning, but it certainly wasn't a remedy I could use often or for the long term. As with most of the things I tried, the results were short-lived at best and my stuttering continued to become more of an embarrassment. I noticed that, sometimes, when I was trying to get a word out, I'd involuntarily start raising my foot, then a leg. The more I struggled to get the word out, the higher the leg would go. Finally, I'd spit the word out and slam my foot to the ground simultaneously, my face becoming beet red. One night, I was watching "The Tonight Show" where Johnny Carson's guest was Mel Tillis, who had a speech impediment of his own. Tillis performed a song flawlessly, but when he sat down beside Johnny I cringed watching him converse. It made me wonder how much people were cringing at me. Or laughing.

I needed to do something, and one evening I saw an "Entertainment Tonight" profile piece on Lester Hayes, the great Oakland Raider cornerback. He'd had a terrible stutter, and he talked about how he had overcome it at a place called the Hollins Communications Research Institute in Roanoke, Virginia. If the Hollins Institute was good enough for Lester Hayes, I figured it was good enough for me. In time, I would come to learn that among HCRI's 5,600-plus client base are John Stossel of ABC's 20/20; Annie Glenn, wife of Ohio Senator and Astronaut John Glenn; and Arthur Blank, co-founder of Home Depot and owner of the Atlanta Falcons.

In retrospect, I can see now that even with my secrets and my lack of self-esteem, there was something inside of me back then that made me feel as if I was worthy of self-improvement. I might not have always been able to conjure up a lot of self-confidence as often as I might need it, but I had drive. From where did this drive come? It certainly didn't come from my mother.

At any rate, I couldn't allow the stuttering to go any further. I saved my money and flew down to Virginia in November of 1977, staying across the street from the Institute at the Hitching Post Motel. The program ran for twenty-eight days and was ten hours a day. There were eight of us in the class. The therapy included speaking in front of the group, speaking in front of a mirror, sounding out words and sentences so that each syllable would last at least two seconds, and lots of breathing exercises. Finally, we had to interact with people publicly, walking up to strangers on the street and asking for directions or the time, and calling up restaurants and asking about hours and dinner specials.

On graduation day, I left the Hollins Institute speaking fluently. I also left with the idea that I wasn't quite ready to go back to Southie just yet.

# CHAPTER EIGHT
# **FLORIDA**

I'm going to work so that it's a pure guts race at the end,
and if it is, I am the only one who can win it.

– STEVE PREFONTAINE –

The Hollins program ended on a Friday and I hitched a ride the next day to Tennessee with a classmate who was driving home. While in high school, I'd written to swim coaches at universities with elite swim programs. I'd never forgotten the remark I'd overheard from the part-time swim coach at the Boys Club: "Tiny's good for around here." I'd wanted to compete with the best. Anywhere. The University of Tennessee swim team was a perennial NCAA powerhouse, always finishing in the top four. The coach was Ray Bussard, and he'd been named Coach of the Year in 1972. I'd written to him and he'd written back. In fact, he'd even sent me a birthday card, or at least the UT athletics department had and he'd either signed it or had someone sign it for him. But of course, I'd settled on Bridgewater.

While in Roanoke I'd somehow managed to scrape up the courage to call Coach Bussard. I told him who I was and where. I told him that

I'd had a couple of bumps along the road and had left Bridgewater, but now I was thinking of coming to Tennessee, or at least hoping I could visit. My dream of getting to the Olympics was still alive, but to this day I have no idea where I got the nerve to pick up the phone and call Coach Bussard. He took the call and said he'd remembered our correspondence, though maybe he was just being kind. He said he'd be happy to meet with me. "Come on down and see me Monday morning and we'll chat," he said.

It was late afternoon when I got dropped off in Knoxville that Saturday, and it so happened that the Tennessee Volunteer football team had just won a home game in front of a sellout crowd and the town was abuzz. I checked into the motel that Coach Bussard had recommended, and then I walked around campus, at one point sneaking into the empty football stadium and going onto the field and launching a make-believe pass towards the end zone. Then I ran down the field like a wide receiver, pretending to hear the crowd cheering me as I caught the air ball and dashed into the end zone for a Volunteer touchdown. It was harmless fun, but looking back, it also strikes me as a microcosm of my penchant for inventing temporary worlds I could live and prosper in.

Eventually, I came across the school's natatorium. There was both an indoor and an outdoor pool, and the outdoor pool was bordered at one end by a stone wall that I walked on top of. Then I sat on the wall and let a shoe drop to the surface of the pool deck, giving me an excuse to have to climb down. Once on the deck, I walked over and touched the water, which seemed somehow important to do. The Hollins Institute had created a newfound confidence. The water in that pool represented another temporary world, one where I could compete and strive to win. *I can do this,* I thought, *and I can do it the right way.* Second Timothy 2:5 came to mind: *Similarly, anyone who competes as an athlete does not receive the victor's crown except by competing according to the rules.*

The next day, I hung around the campus. As I walked back to the motel later that night, a male student and two coeds passed by me on their way to the dorms. One of the girls pointed to me as they walked past and said to the other girl, "What about him? He's cute." They kept walking, and I thought of all the clever things I wished I could have said. "And available," I imagined myself boldly saying back to them with a big charming smile. But I couldn't say anything. What I really wished was that they hadn't seen me at all.

I stayed again Sunday night at the motel, and on Monday morning I went to see Coach Bussard. Walking down what seemed like a mile-long corridor to his office, I couldn't help but notice all the pictures on the walls of current and former Tennessee Volunteer swimming stars—NCAA champions and All-Americans and even Olympic medal winners. It was inspiring, if not a bit intimidating. A kid from Southie? *Here?* But if I had any second thoughts about being there, they were trumped by the idea that this is what I knew I really wanted. What I hoped on hope to make a reality. Maybe Coach Bussard would tell me to get lost, and maybe a big part of me was sure that he would, but at least I had made it this far.

But then everything seemed to unravel the moment he introduced himself to me in his office. It took me what seemed like several minutes just to stammer out my reply: "H-H-H-i, I-I-I-I'm F-F-F-Fran." *Oh, God, please help me get my name out.* This, less than three days after completing the intense, twenty-eight-day program at Hollins. I'd remained stutter-free for less than seventy-two hours.

Coach Bussard waited patiently for me to make it through my introduction and then asked me something about whether the motel accommodations had been adequate. In my head, I tried hard to make light of the situation, thinking, *you just saw how long it took me to say three words and you want to ask me* another *question?! Are you nuts?* With this little bit of refocusing, I somehow managed to get something out and then the coach excused himself to have a word with his secretary right outside his door. I sat in his office certain that he was trying to find a graceful way to get rid of the idiotic kid who'd found his way into his office. But instead, he came back in and smiled and said, "Come on, I'll show you around."

Coach Bussard drove us around the campus with him doing most of the talking, pointing out various buildings and athletics facilities. At one point, we drove by the Hearing and Speech Center, which is located on what is today Peyton Manning Pass and he said, "If you come here, you can continue to work on your speech right there."

From time to time, Coach Bussard would ask me questions about my background and family, patiently and kindly waiting for my answers. Soon, I was feeling comfortable with him. "I don't really know my dad," I said. "My mom probably drinks too much." I'm not sure exactly why I felt comfortable, but I did have the thought that this is what I'd always wanted. I wanted a chance. I needed help and didn't know how to ask for it. Coach Bussard was in a position to provide that help, and on some level, I knew—or at least hoped—that I was ready to accept it.

I remained at UT for the next two days, staying in the athletics dorm on campus. Forty-eight hours was as long as the NCAA would allow a school to host a recruit. While I was there, Coach Bussard let me sit in on practices, and also had me take the ACT test to find out where I was academically. I guess he discovered I needed to put in some work. "If you come here," he told me, "I'll get you in for the new semester in January, next month. But you're going to have to work hard at your studies. Really hard. If your grades are good, you can try out for the team the next fall."

On the return flight to Boston, I thought to myself, *you can do this,* and for a few days, I basked in the opportunity and how blessed I was to have it. I shared the possibilities with Gram and a few close friends. But one day, walking in the cold to my mother's house from the Club, it hit me that I would not be going to Tennessee. I was still carrying around my awful secret. If I went to Tennessee and my secret somehow got out, I'd be too ashamed to stick around and I hated the thought of having to leave such a promising place. Coach Bussard had been so kind to me, and the athletes I'd met in the dorm were encouraging and supportive. The people on campus, like the two girls who'd made the remark about me as they'd passed by me, all seemed fun and nice. This was the place for my dreams to become reality…and the kind of place where you could get close to people. Too close. Closeness meant sharing and sharing meant risk.

My grandmother made the decision easier: Tennessee was in the South, a world removed from Boston, and not just by miles. Down there, it was different than it was in New England. Gram wasn't comfortable with the idea of me going away to a place she perceived as being so dissimilar to the world she knew. Within two weeks of being home, any idea I'd had of going to Tennessee was gone. That next fall, in what could have been my first year on the team, the Tennessee Volunteers would win the 1978 NCAA Swimming Championship. Coach Bussard would win his second Coach of the Year award.

In the meantime, I felt panic. Now what would I do? Where would I go? I couldn't stay in Southie. I couldn't stand being around my mother or Frankie. But then I thought of Miami, Florida. Another coach I'd written to was the coach of the University of Miami's swim team. Miami suddenly seemed like a good possibility to me. A lot of friends had gone on spring break there. It was sunny and warm. Realistically, as far as my issues were concerned, there wasn't much difference between the two schools except that absolutely nobody knew me in Miami. I knew Miami only in the abstract. It was just a concept, a far-off place where I was hopeful I could blend in and get lost. The problem with Tennessee was that it had become all too real. Of course, it never really occurred to me that the same thing would happen at Miami. Not to mention that for all I knew the coach could have quit, moved, or retired. Of course, what Miami really represented was an immediate escape plan.

Gram didn't care for Miami any more than she cared for Tennessee. When she saw how serious I was about the idea, she asked me if I would at least talk it over with Father Phinney at St. Monica's Church. Father Phinney didn't like the idea, either. "You belong here, with your grandmother," he told me. "This is your home, not Tennessee and not Miami. Miami is a city full of sin."

These were the exact wrong words to say to a young single man. Suddenly, Miami seemed even more exotic and alluring than before. Still, I was sure Father Phinney was exaggerating, and I found myself resenting him for it, resenting the idea that he felt he had to talk down to me, that he felt he needed to embellish instead of just speak to me man to man. What I needed was guidance—somebody to help me make an important life decision, not a blunt admonition. I needed somebody to help me think through the choice I was about to make. How will you afford it? Will you be able to get a job? Will you have time to study? Will you be willing to stick with it? These were the considerations I needed help with; I didn't need someone telling me what was good for me and what wasn't. What wasn't, was staying in Southie.

And there was one more factor in my decision to go. Beth and I had broken up by then. I had hoped for something long-lasting with Beth. I had tried to be open to her, but, hell, I didn't know how to be open with anybody. Even so, I thought we might be able to somehow get back together. But one night before Christmas, Beth came over to visit Gram and me. It was a nice visit, but there was a distance between us. Before she left, she and I sat down and she shared with me that she was pregnant. It wasn't mine. We talked some more and cried together, and then she went home. Now there really wasn't anything keeping me in Southie. The next day, I made the decision to go.

Three days after Christmas, I flew down to Miami. I got off the airplane into the warm sunshine and noticed palm trees everywhere. *Oh, yeah!* Unlike with Tennessee, I hadn't called the coach ahead of time. I took a bus to the Coral Gables campus only to learn that the coach had moved on. He was now at Miami-Dade Community College in Kendall. I stuck around UM for the day and checked out the swimming facilities. Greg Louganis was there, diving. He'd transferred to Miami that year. He wasn't yet a household name, but I'd remembered watching him in the 1976 Olympics. He was sure to be a favorite for gold in 1980 at the Moscow games.

I spent the first couple nights in Miami at the airport, sleeping in a chair, pretending that I was waiting for a plane or that I'd missed one. I didn't have a lot of money, and I needed to make it last. An aunt and uncle had kindly given me a fifty-dollar bill when I'd approached them for some help, telling them that I was traveling to Florida. My plan was to hold onto it as tightly as I could. I knew that once I broke it, it wouldn't last long.

On the third night, I finally got a room at a motel across from UM. The next day, I took a bus to Kendall to check out the swimming facilities and maybe meet the coach with whom I'd assumed I had corresponded, but it was New Year's Eve and everything was closed. I walked around the campus a bit and then I went back to the motel only to find a lockbox on my door. A kid younger than me was working the front desk.

"You haven't paid for last night," he said. "I can't let you back in the room until you settle the bill."

"But my money's in my room," I said. I had the fifty in my pocket but I didn't see any reason to let the clerk know that.

"Sorry, man, I don't make the rules. If you can come up with what you owe, I can let you in. But I can't let you in until then. I'd get fired."

There were other people hanging around the lobby, one of whom was a woman whose provocative manner of dress suggested lady of the evening. She'd overheard the conversation, and she walked up to the desk clerk and took his hand. "Sweetie, I think you can let this nice young man into his room," she smiled, turning and winking in my direction. "You can trust him. He looks like a good soul. Don't you think so?"

The clerk hemmed and hawed but gave in and walked me back to my room where he took off the lock and then turned and went back to the lobby. I stayed in the room the rest of the night, getting some sleep and waking around 4:30 a.m. Then I packed up my things and left, the fifty-dollar bill still in my pocket.

# CHAPTER NINE
# FINDING MYSELF

Start where you are. Use what you have. Do what you can.

– ARTHUR ASHE –

I spent New Year's Day and night back at the Miami airport. On the second, I went back to the Kendall campus, determined to enroll. On a bulletin board, I found a note advertising a room for rent. Before taking the bus back to Miami airport where I assumed I would be spending the night, and despite my fears of stuttering through a phone conversation, I called the number on the note. The room was in a three-bedroom condo on Kendall Drive and it came with a bed and linens. Two guys a couple of years older than me lived there and they accepted my fifty-dollar bill as a deposit on the rent.

On the third, I went looking for a job. I had told my new roommates that my family back in Boston was mailing some money to me from which I'd be able to pay the balance of the rent. "My grandmother didn't want me traveling with a lot of money," I explained. Of course, there was no money coming.

Within walking distance of the condo was Kelly's Seafood House and they were looking for help. I had kitchen experience, and besides the money, I knew if I got a job at a restaurant, I wouldn't go hungry. I prayed not to stutter through my interview. The kitchen manager was on vacation and I was interviewed by two other managers, Pete and Tom. It helped my confidence that we talked while seated at a table where I could put my feet under my chair; I knew Pete and Tom wouldn't be able to see my foot rising upwards if I started to stammer. I managed to make it through the interview and they offered me a job as a baker.

A week later, when the kitchen manager returned, she walked up and introduced herself. I was in the back of the house working, and her appearance startled me. I couldn't get so much as a syllable out, never mind my name. Janet waited patiently for a little while and then graciously excused herself, saying something like, "Well, it's nice to meet you," and then retreated into her kitchen office. I would find out later, after we'd all become good friends and could laugh about it, that Janet had approached Pete and Tom afterward and said, "Are you guys f--king kidding me?! This is who you hired? He can't even talk!" Pete and Tom had no idea what she was referring to.

Overall, my speech had become much improved, but in moments like that, moments when I was taken by surprise, I backslid. I didn't handle surprises well. I still don't. I often jump if somebody comes up from behind me. Thinking back on that four-year-old in the cellar of my grandparents' house, it's not hard to imagine why.

For six weeks, I lied to my roommates while I saved my money, giving them excuses, at one point telling them that the Blizzard of '78, which had serendipitously hit New England that year, had prevented my grandmother from getting to the post office. Any day now, I kept telling them. By then, I was enrolled in school, attending 5:30 a.m. swim practice, and working, so they came to trust me. They knew I wasn't going anywhere. Eventually, I saved enough of my wages from Kelly's to make rent.

At school, I joined the swim team. Coach Errol Seegers was a burly guy, Hemingway-like in both body and spirit. He took a liking to me. Said I had "moxie." Swim practice was twice a day—5:30 in the morning and 5:30 in the evening. In the meantime, I took a part-time, work-study job in the school's AV department. With classes, swimming, and two jobs, there wasn't a lot of free time, and that was okay with me, at least for the time being. I enjoyed being busy and I just focused on doing what I liked the most—blending into the crowd as best I could.

At Kelly's, I made some good friends and had a lot of laughs. I moved up to a cook position in the back of the house and then to cook in the front of the house. I became close friends with a fellow cook named Jack, and we started playing tennis together. On the swim team, I worked hard but had limited success in the meets. Still—naively—I had the 1980 Olympics on my mind.

Through 1978 and 1979, I worked and swam and went to classes. I kept in touch with Kathy and Gram back home and, only on occasion, with Ma. One time, I was telling Kathy about my boss and now good friend Janet. Janet, as it turned out, wanted to become a man. "I guess she's gay," I said. "Can you believe it?"

"Hey, don't knock it till you've tried it," Kathy replied. I took the phone away from my ear and looked at it in disbelief. *Did I just hear that right? Is Kathy gay? My sister?* She'd been married by then with two sons, but she'd gotten divorced and I knew her husband had been abusive. In fact, Kathy had a history of being with abusive men. I didn't ask any more questions of Kathy that day, but, in time, I would learn that, yes, she'd become a lesbian. Or maybe she'd been a lesbian all along but, the childhood she'd endured, complete with Frankie's sexual abuse and going back even further—Kathy would reveal to me years later that she'd been molested by that police captain who was our foster father back in Natick—didn't do anything to kindle any kind of fondness or trust for men.

In September of '79, I found myself shaken by an incident at Kelly's that would cause me to rethink being away from home. After hours one night, Jack and I were closing along with Janet and Donna, another manager. We were hanging out in the office having a beer. I was sitting in a chair by the door when a man in a Halloween mask walked in. I thought it must have been one of the dishwashers goofing around. "Little early for Halloween, isn't it?" I said. Then the man shoved the barrel of a shotgun into my side. Another guy came in behind the first, and after opening the safe, we were ordered to the floor, Jack and I directed to lie face down next to each other and the girls to lie across us in the other direction. Then our hands were tied, and the robbers cleaned out the safe and instructed us not to call the police for ten minutes. Then they left. When the police were finally called, they suggested that it might have been an inside job. The four of us had a few more drinks talking to them and thinking, an inside job? *Really? Look at us.* A few weeks later, the robbers were caught. They'd pulled off the same heist at a few different restaurants around town. My mind was a blur during the robbery, and I have only a vague recollection of what happened as we lay there tied up, but Jack would later laugh about how fast I had kept repeating the Hail Mary. Apparently, there had been no stuttering then.

The robbery tainted my view of my life in Miami, and something else a few months later would prove to be the final straw, ultimately sending me back to Southie. In February of 1980, Jimmy Carter made good on his promise to boycott the Olympic Games in Moscow if the USSR would not pull out of Afghanistan. Though it had been an extraordinarily naive dream—I didn't even know where the trials were being held or anything at all about the process—it had been my whole reason for being in Miami, my whole reason for being away from home. Or maybe it was my excuse. My escape. Either way, as unrealistic as it might have been, my Olympic dream had been the one thing on my mind that had provided me with any kind of motivation to get up each morning and out the door.

I hung around through the winter and returned to Southie in April of 1980. With no real idea of what to do next with my life, or even where to live, I hooked up with some buddies of mine who were pooling their money to rent a house on Chappaquiddick for the summer. There were six of us and the plan was to live there from Memorial Day to Labor Day. Two of the guys only came down over a few weekends, but Sean Martin, Michael Henry, Richie Faith (one of Michael Faith's younger brothers), and I were there pretty much the whole time. We took menial jobs, just enough to give us some spending cash. It was an entire summer of going to the beach, parties, and laughter. We'd play cards all night and listen to music. Friends visited throughout the summer. And we met other summer people. One girl's father owned a liquor store and kept sending her and her sister bottles of Jack Daniels that we helped them drink.

I eventually left sometime in August, going back to Southie. I couldn't drink anymore, not even a beer. I was restless. I needed physical activity. I needed to move. We swam on occasion. Sometimes we'd swim the short route back to Chappaquiddick if we'd gone into Edgartown and missed the last ferry of the day. I biked sometimes around town or would go for a mile- or two-mile run here and there, but I missed the discipline of regular physical workouts. There were some wonderful tennis clubs around Boston that I wanted to play at, too. I wasn't very good, but I enjoyed learning the sport. All in all, the practice and competition helped keep the demons at bay.

Later that year, I went to work at the Gillette factory packing razors. The plant was in South Boston, and most of my family had worked there at one time or another. Outside of restaurants, it seemed like the only place I could get a job with a steady income. By then, I wasn't very much concerned with the future. I was twenty-four and had it in my mind that I'd surely be dead by the age of twenty-eight. I didn't really know how it would come about, and I wasn't spending any time wishing for it; it was just a feeling that I had. Deep down, I couldn't imagine surviving much longer than that with my secret, with my shame.

Frankie worked at Gillette, too, although he worked the day shift. I eventually took a third-shift job, which suited me well. I was splitting time between Ma's place and my grandmother's place, where Frankie still lived. By then, he'd divorced Diane. The marriage hadn't lasted two years. Working late meant avoiding Ma at the worst time of the day for her drinking, as well as avoiding Frankie at night.

Frankie by then had moved upstairs to what had been my aunts' room. I still slept in the cellar when I was there, and although Frankie hadn't tried anything since that day I had told him "no more," I still tried to sleep lightly, hoping I'd be able to hear him if he came down the steps. I continued to spend nights at friends' places, too. Sometimes, Frankie would get upset, saying he would worry about me if I didn't come home. "I'm just fine, thank you," I'd say. I knew his concern was bulls--t. But Frankie and I were civil and even friendly. I imagine the situation was more awkward for me than him. I was still encouraging him to get his GED. I was still trying to ignore all that had happened, still trying to stuff the secret, still hoping that maybe it would all go the f--k away and not matter anymore.

Meanwhile, I was becoming closer to my nephews, Kathy's two boys Matthew and Michael. Kathy was living in Dorchester, just a couple of streets over from our old place on Rawson Street. I'd visit the kids often. I'd babysit them and make dinner for them. I'd let them stay up late and we'd watch movies and eat popcorn. They had no regular father figure in their lives. I knew what that was about, and maybe I was becoming something of that to them.

In the fall of 1981, I enrolled in an Outward Bound program. Twenty-six days of sailing, hiking, camping, and rock climbing on and around Hurricane Island and Penobscot Bay in Maine. It seemed important, once again, to get out of my comfort zone. Looking back, I suppose, in some way, I was trying to find myself, to discover what or who I was supposed to be. A lot of the time was spent on a thirty-foot open sailboat called *Serendipity* with ten other students, sailing around the rugged Maine coast. One day, it rained hard and it kept on raining.

We were far enough out where we couldn't even see land. I was wet and cold and miserable and I had the thought that I could die out there. Part of me wanted to. Another part knew I wouldn't, and that realization came along with the idea that if I was destined to live, then I needed to do something with my life, though I had no idea what. A thought crossed my mind briefly that maybe what this was all about was that I was supposed to learn how to overcome. Overcome my own fears and insecurities. Overcome myself. Could it be that a belief in myself was evolving? Learn to trust God and just be. But of course, I didn't know how, and in my gloom, I pulled out my harmonica and began to play "Michael Row Your Boat Ashore," one of two songs I knew, the other being "I've Been Working on the Railroad." Soon, the other people on the boat began humming along and tapping their feet, and the whole mood of the boat seemed to shift.

One morning before breakfast, we were gathered on a large rock on Hurricane Island for the daily spiritual/motivational lesson. The instructor read us Jenny Joseph's poem "Warning": "When I am an old woman I shall wear purple / With a red hat which doesn't go, and doesn't suit me," the poem begins. It's probably best known for being the inspiration behind the "Red Hat Society," an international society of older women, but the poem is about doing things now, instead of waiting until it doesn't really matter. And again, I was hit with the idea that I should be doing something with my life. Wasn't it possible, after all, that I might survive beyond twenty-eight? It inspired me temporarily, but I knew that moments of inspiration were always fleeting for me. And so I continued to imagine that twenty-eight would be it.

Thanksgiving morning, Old Harbor projects.

Kathy and me,
outside 96 O'Callaghan Way.

With Ma.

Halfball strike zone.

Kathy and me with Ma, 96 O'Callaghan Way, Old Harbor projects.

19 Knowlton Street.

Me and Kathy, Rawson Street.

Kathy and me.

Ma, Kathy, and me outside of Great Grandma's in
the Old Harbor projects, dressed for First Holy Communion.

Old Harbor projects. Front: Jackie, me, Michael (RIP),
Back: Florence, Georgie, Ma, Kathy

D Street Projects. Front: Michael, me, Danny.
Back: Jackie, Georgie, Florence, Kathy.

Dorchester Heights behind
South Boston High School.

Southie High.

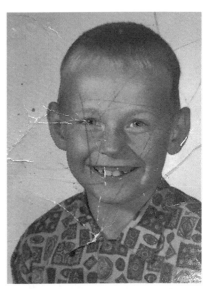

Did I scribble my face out in this one?

Gram (Peg) and Grandpa (Frank).

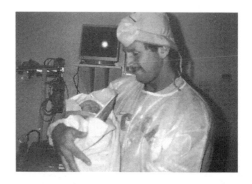

The birth of Sam, June 27, 1989, 2:24pm.
Seven pounds, five ounces, twenty inches.

Lobsters in Maine with Sam.

With Sam in Southie, Castle Island.

With Sam in Saint Patrick's
Cathedral, Dublin.

With Gina and Sam.

My friend Annie still works at the Club, forty-plus years later.
It was Annie who lent me her car to go to my first triathlon in 1982.

With Dave McGillivray (Foreword).

Triathlon racing in South Boston USTS, 1985.

Racing as a member of the Saucony Triathlon Racing Team.

With Sam, Boston 2013,
the day before the Marathon bombings.

With Sam and Gina, returning to the Boston Marathon in 2014 to
run and support Boston Strong and Team MR8 for Martin Richard
family. Martin was eight when he was killed in the bombing.

# CHAPTER TEN
# FORGETTING

Did you really think sealing me in concrete and burying
me in the yard was even going to slow me down?!

– RANMA –

Sometime in August of 1982, a friend of mine named Mark Thomas introduced me to the idea of triathlon competitions—races that include swimming, biking, and running. I knew Mark from the Boys Club. The previous summer, I had filled in for Mark as aquatics instructor at the club, since he had a summer job. I was immediately intrigued by the idea of triathlon competition and, within two weeks of Mark mentioning the idea to me, I signed myself up for a triathlon in Medford that I saw advertised in the *Boston Globe*. The Bay State Triathlon was a mile swim, forty-mile bike, and ten-mile run. I'd done some swimming at the Club, of course. I'd also done some swimming at nearby Pleasure Bay, which the Southie locals called "the lagoon," and some open-water swims from JFK Library and the L Street Bathhouse. I'd also done some biking around town, along with a little running around Columbus Park, but nothing that you could classify as serious training.

I borrowed my friend Annie's car, and Michael Faith came along for moral support. I did okay. The ten-mile-run part of the race was a five-mile loop that you had to circle twice, and by the second time around, I was walking. Michael found me along the route and cheered me on. In the end, out of a hundred or so entrants, I came in thirty-third.

That I managed to finish at all was remarkable to me, and the experience was encouraging. I found myself with a pursuit that I began feeling a passion for. I started training and regularly entered other triathlons that popped up around New England. I met and befriended other runners and triathletes, including a guy named Bob Clark, who worked at the Southie post office. He invited me out to Boston College where there was a group of other runners called the Master Runners and I was able to train with them on the track, learning a lot in the process, not only from Bob and the other great runners, but by listening in when BC coach Jack McDonald spoke to them. A big part of the appeal, of course, was that the training gave me something positive to focus on, something that could help crowd out all the noise between my ears. But it also gave me something I could try to excel at. I wasn't ever going to be an Olympic swimmer, but I could work at being a decent triathlete. I started feeling that spark again that I had lost in Miami, if not before.

After Gillette, I bounced around at other jobs including kitchen and bartending jobs at the Royal Sonesta hotel, the Hilton, and the Boston Athletic Club. I worked at the Hilton as a line cook, before getting a terrific break from Paul Buckley, the general manager, who promoted me to sous-chef.

I was gambling, too. I bet on basketball and football games. One time, I lost several hundred dollars on a parlay, betting four basketball teams to win and at the last minute adding a fifth—Phoenix—to the bet. It was a move made from a desire for self-reliance, along with some greed. I wanted to become rich because if I became rich, maybe things would change. I'd been doing well blending in and living a life that looked normal from the outside, but I'd come to the conclusion somewhere along the line that being normal wasn't enough. Being a good guy wasn't enough. Being liked, even being loved, wasn't enough. If I was going to rise above the hiding and the shame of my secret, I needed to be somebody really great. If I were rich enough, I could be anybody. I could change my name and go somewhere else. Maybe *then*, I could forget the secret. It would be as if none of it had ever happened.

Anyway, all four teams but Phoenix won. I managed to pay off the bet but stayed mad at myself for days—not for betting, but for over-thinking the bet and being greedy and adding the extra team to the parlay. Not long after came another bet and this one I couldn't pay off right away. I was down three hundred dollars, and I got a visit one day in the kitchen of the Boston Athletic Club from a no-nonsense guy named Pat. "You owe us money, Fran," he said quietly. "You're late with it. When are you going to pay?" Much later I would learn that Pat's last name was Nee. Even later, I would learn that Pat Nee was part-ners with Whitey Bulger, the mobster whom Kevin Weeks—the guy I knew who used to dive on our swim team at the Boys Club—worked for. Pat had started in a rival gang but, eventually, he and Bulger had formed an alliance. Bulger had his hands in everything, getting a take everywhere. I didn't know of Pat's connection to Bulger at the time, or of any of his connections, but he put a scare into me that day at the Boston Athletic Club. I'd never had anybody approach me about a bet before and Pat made an intimidating presence. It was just him and me in that kitchen. He gave me another deadline and I made sure I wasn't a second late.

Pat was actually friendly to me. We started to get to know each other at the Athletic Club, and one day we got to talking about my interest in triathlons, which was something he said he wanted to try. Still having no idea of his connections, I offered to help him. Soon, we were training together—swimming, biking, and running with another friend named Steve. Over the course of the next couple of summers, Pat and Steve and I entered events all over New England—in Maine, New Hampshire, Connecticut, Vermont, everywhere. Pat occasionally helped with expenses, especially if the event was out of town or required an overnight stay.

I still had no idea of his connections, nor did I ask very many questions, but one time he confided to me that he was part of a gang that he wanted to get out of but couldn't.

"How come?" I asked.

"You wouldn't understand, Fran," he said. "A gang like this, you just can't leave."

"Yeah, but if you don't want to be in it..."

"I know too much."

"Huh? Like what?"

Pat just smiled, and that was pretty much the end of our conversation about the gang. Many years later, I would find out it was Whitey Bulger he was with. Not long after that conversation, we were doing a long bike ride from Boston to Cape Cod when an eighteen-wheeler got a little too close. Pat shot the driver the finger as he went past, and the driver slowed down; soon, the two of them were jawing at each other and hurling obscenities back and forth. Then the trucker pulled over. Pat got off his bike and started walking towards him.

"Pat," I said, "come on. This guy isn't worth any trouble. Let's just keep going." But Pat kept walking towards the truck, wearing his cycling cleats, which don't give a guy much better balance or traction than high heels would. The trucker, a brawny guy with big shoulders, came down from his cab and strode towards Pat. Things didn't look good, and I wondered what my role was going to be. Would I have to jump in and help Pat if the trucker started to get the upper hand? Soon, the two were face to face, still jawing at each other. Then, in an instant, out of nowhere, Pat drove a fist hard into the trucker's face. The trucker crumpled to the ground and knelt there for a couple of long moments. Pat bent over him and then grabbed him by the back of the head and said something to him while gradually helping him to his feet. The trucker nodded, turned, and walked gingerly back to his truck and soon drove off.

"Geez, Pat," I said, "what did you say to him?"

"I told him who my associates were," he said. I laughed and didn't ask who. If he was serious, I really didn't want to know.

Sometime around those years, Pat helped Whitey Bulger organize a plan to smuggle guns to the IRA. They bought a boat and filled it with weapons and hired some IRA sympathizers to sail it to Ireland. One of them, John McIntyre, ended up talking to the authorities. Later, Pat, unknowingly set up by Bulger, brought McIntyre to his brother's house where Bulger was waiting for him. Pat left the house to attend to business and when he came back, he learned Bulger had tortured and killed McIntyre. I didn't have a clue any of this was going on, or about any of the other crimes Pat was involved in. It was the same level of naivety that I'd had about being an Olympian, and it probably saved me here. Pat Nee and I eventually went our separate ways. I stuck with triathlons. Pat stuck with whatever it was he was doing.

In the fall of 1982, three days shy of the six-year anniversary of my grandfather's death, I lost my grandmother. She was seventy-one and her health unexpectedly went south. I knew she'd never really gotten over the loss of my grandfather, but I also knew that Gram had begun drinking her daily nightcap a little earlier and it was lasting a little longer. Even during her illness, I never imagined her drinking was that bad, of course. Nor, apparently, did her sisters Mary and Helen, and they would often share dinner and weekends together.

At the Carney hospital, where she eventually was taken, I held Gram's hand as she passed. There was some involuntary muscle movement immediately afterward, and I thought for a moment that maybe she hadn't died. I cried out to the nurse, but Gram was gone. I bought a nice new suit for her funeral and it made me feel sharp until Uncle Larry saw me and laughed and said, "Who do you think *you* are? You look ridiculous in that, Tiny." I decided I didn't care what Uncle Larry thought. I knew Gram would have loved seeing me in the suit, and I was there for her.

Meanwhile, competing in triathlons continued to be a very good thing for me. Somewhere in 1983, I introduced myself to Dave McGillivray, whom I had seen at many of the best running events around Boston. It was Dave who put on the Medford Bay State Triathlon. Dave had an amazing background and is still amazing to this day. I've been encouraged by his work, family, and friendship. In 1978, he'd run across the United States, from Medford, Oregon, to Medford, Massachusetts, raising money for cancer research. The total distance was close to 3,500 miles. In 1980, he ran 1,520 miles from Winter Haven, Florida, to Boston, also for cancer. He was accompanied by Bob Hall, the first man to complete the Boston Marathon in a wheelchair. The two stopped at the White House along the way and met Jimmy Carter. In 1982, Dave ran the Boston Marathon blindfolded to raise money for the Carroll Center for the Blind in Newtown, Massachusetts.

I eventually learned that Dave worked for Saucony running shoes as director of promotions. Whenever I saw him, I always tried to say hello, hoping I wouldn't stutter. Eventually, I would ask him if and how I could try out for the Saucony Triathlon Racing Team. Dave would allow me to join for the 1985 season, and I would end up on the team for the '86 season, too. Having Saucony sponsor me meant free shoes and team gear. I won a couple of the smaller Massachusetts races in that period, one of which was the Equalizer, held in and around Lynn, Swampscott, and Nahant, Massachusetts. The Equalizer consisted of a four-mile swim, fifty-five-mile bike race, and fifteen-mile run. I had a support group that day—Tom and Ray, a couple of friends of mine. My nephews Matty and Michael were there, too. Nana, my grandmother on my father's side, came. Even Ma was there, joined by her boyfriend Bernie.

Ma and Bernie had shown up to see me in a triathlon in 1984 in Lake Placid. I liked Bernie. He was a nice guy and was good to Ma. Ma had had a variety of boyfriends; there always seemed to be somebody. Bernie was the most serious one, but like the others, he eventually left, probably because he couldn't keep up with Ma's drinking. Few men could.

The training for the triathlons and the competition continued to teach me the value of consistency and perseverance. These traits would prove to be priceless later on when I would need them the most. I started, in fact, to become attuned to the concept of perseverance, seeing it in little metaphorical examples in my everyday life. On a November Saturday in 1984, I was working the bar at the Royal Sonesta hotel. The Boston College football game was on. We'd get celebrities in the bar from time to time and that day "Marvelous" Marvin Hagler came in wearing a long fur coat, his entourage in tow. Under normal circumstances, that might have been the most memorable thing for me that day. But the Boston College game had been a wild, back-and-forth, high-scoring affair, and the place had become raucous. I'd noticed one older Boston College alumni in a wheelchair rooting for B.C. all game long but giving up towards the end as the University of Miami took the lead with barely any time left. He paid his tab and left in complete disgust. He was probably in the parking lot when Doug Flutie threw his famous Hail Mary pass into Gerard Phelan's hands in the end zone for the win as time expired. The Royal Sonesta went crazy (most of Boston, too) and I remember thinking what a shame the guy in the wheelchair couldn't have hung in there for just a couple more minutes to see one of the all-time great moments in sports.

I took a lesson from that experience, one of a couple different lessons around that time. When I started working at the Hilton, the general manager gave me a book called *The Greatest Salesman in the World* by Og Mandino, about a poor camel boy who achieved a life of abundance. The boy followed the principles of ten scrolls with sage advice like, "All is worthless without action," and "I will persist until I succeed." There were good and healthy influences all around me, and looking back, it seems clear that I was open to them, even if I didn't accept them all.

Part of me wanted to rise above my past, but a bigger part of me still held out hope I'd be able to just forget it. Bury it and forget it. *Move on,* I kept telling myself. *Keep moving.* In my mind, forgetting was the only way to move past the secret and the shame. And I could forget it all if I could just be a good athlete, a good friend, a good worker, a good guy. In short, if I could just change my life, I could change myself. The sexual abuse? It would be as if it never even happened.

Naturally, it wouldn't let me go. I could not forget, no matter what I did, no matter where I went, no matter who I was. Sometimes, I would scream out loud in frustration. *F--k, just let me go!* As deep down as I tried to push it, shove it, stuff it, I could not keep it from haunting me. When twenty-eight came and went and I was still alive, I figured now what? I guess I'd just have to try even harder to forget.

# CHAPTER ELEVEN
# TO THE SURFACE

Writing is like a 'lust,' or like 'scratching when you itch.'
Writing comes as a result of a very strong impulse,
and when it does come, I, for one, must get it out.

– C. S. Lewis –

In August of 1985, on a long bike ride with five other cyclists, I was hit by a car. We had just finished a brief hydration/fuel stop, and I was bringing up the rear of our group when an elderly driver, who later claimed he hadn't seen me, hit me from behind. I fell forward into the street and had the sensation of the car's right front tire rolling over my shoulder and the side of my head. The thought struck me that *now* I was going to die, after I'd finally found something in life I enjoyed, like triathlons to compete in and practice for. The impact broke my humerus, but I was alive. My upper arm was in a cast for several weeks, and I didn't know quite how to feel. Grateful to be alive, I supposed, but I'd never been injured before. How was I supposed to deal with that?

There was a court trial, but I made an awful witness. First of all, the case didn't reach the courtroom for months, and by then, I was out of the cast and in full training for triathlons, gradually getting back into racing form. To maintain my sponsorship with Saucony, I'd felt the need to heal quickly, to resume my training, and to continue to try to improve my race times. I had hopes of going to Kona, Hawaii for the Ironman World Championship the following year. It was a 2.4-mile swim, 112-mile bike, and 26.2-mile run.

Thinking back, maybe there was even more to it. Since I was going to live, I *needed* the training, needed the sense that I was whole, that there were no ill effects from the accident, the same way I'd always needed all those friends. I needed the affirmation. I needed the sense that at least everything on the outside was okay in my life. Maybe it was more whitewashing. It's hard even now for me to say. Somewhere, somehow, I was hoping to learn more than to just survive. Deep down, I wanted to succeed. I had always wanted that, notwithstanding my secret and my shame. Not everything one does is a means by which to escape. There were a lot of good times in my past, with all of those friends. Music and ballgames and laughter. And there was always a genuine desire to be great at something with my athletic pursuits. Not everything has to be whitewashing, though I acknowledge the lines might blur.

Whatever the motivation, by the time of the trial, I certainly didn't appear to be any worse for wear. I looked healthy and fit. And the sensation I'd had of having my head run over was pretty much dismissed as impossible. I'd have been dead, was the thinking. But that's what I felt and so that's what I'd reported. Worst of all was my performance on the witness stand. I was anxious and stuttering and wiping my sweaty palms on my knees, becoming more and more self-conscious until I finally just couldn't say anything at all. When one of the other cyclists testified that I'd been riding carelessly, that pretty much sealed the deal. The elderly driver got off scot-free. It was infuriating. I knew the accident was not my fault. I hadn't been riding carelessly. The driver was wrong, but because I couldn't speak on the stand, I lost the case.

That year ended on a positive note, however. A couple of months after the accident, I was waiting for the train at Ashmont Station after having visited my brother Danny, who was living around that area. There were two young men about my age who were evangelizing, and I sat and listened to them and soon we were talking. Both were named Tom and they invited me to their house church, which was not far away. I ended up going repeatedly. There was a Monday night service at the house, Wednesday Bible study, and Sunday church services, the Sunday services sometimes held at Boston Garden. This was the Church of Christ, and though it was far different from the Catholicism in which I was raised, it felt right to me. It felt positive. I was reading and studying the Bible and it seemed to give me some spiritual direction and focus, which I had been looking for and lacking until then. Ma didn't like the idea, but on December 18, 1985, I was baptized by the Church of Christ.

The good feeling wouldn't last. The Church helped, but in the end, I was still unable to let go of the past and, therefore, still unable to move on as if the past hadn't happened. I still didn't know where I was headed or what I was going to do with my life. But I kept training for and competing in triathlons. On more than one occasion, the question was raised by the church about my commitment to our Lord and Savior. I knew I was committed, but I also knew that I loved to compete and hoped I could commit to both.

I won a few triathlons that summer of 1986. Next stop: Kona. To help pay for my trip, there was a family and friends fundraising event for me at the Boston Athletic Club, put together by Annie Gordon, Ray Cox, and me. It was Annie's car that I had borrowed four years earlier for that first triathlon in Medford, and Ray drove the support vehicle during the Equalizer Triathlon. The fundraiser event made for a fun night. Dave McGillivray and Hal Gabriel, another Ironman finisher, came and spoke on my behalf, and there was a slideshow, put to music, of a few of the different triathlons I'd competed in. My mother was there, behaving. So was my Uncle Walter, Aunt Helen's husband, known as Walla. Some of my cousins were there as well.

The problem was that in August, I was in another bike accident, almost a year to the day from the first one. A car cut through a line of traffic in front of me to enter into a mall parking lot. He'd been waved through by the other drivers, but he hadn't seen me coming up on the side of the road, and not seeing or expecting him, I ended up slamming into the passenger-side door. I wasn't seriously hurt, although I was taken by ambulance to a hospital. I was released with a prescription for physical therapy. My training came to a temporary halt, but I went out to Hawaii two months later anyway with Dave McGillivray and several other athletes. Annie and Ray came, too.

I did a couple short runs in Hawaii, the first I'd run in two months. I wasn't sure I should enter the triathlon. "Do the swim at least," Dave suggested. "And if you drop out after that, then you drop out." He knew I wouldn't. We both knew. Once I started, I'd have to finish.

I felt good at the start of the Ironman. It felt good just to be in Hawaii, and I'd experienced a little burst of optimism upon the simple act of picking up my race packet. Plus, I became excited when I saw I had a low bib number. Low numbers are usually reserved for the more esteemed athletes. Maybe my low number can do the run for me and I'll wait at the finish line, I joked. It was also a boost to see that my bike was on the same bike rack as four-time Kona champion Dave Scott— wearing bib number two—who would win his fifth Kona championship that day. Still, that was as high as my hopes would reach. After the swim, the shortest in distance and time of the three events, I struggled. There was a heavy crosswind along the bike portion of the race and it seemed as if I was in slow motion. But I finished. At less than thirteen hours, I came in somewhere a little above the middle of the pack.

I returned to Boston, a city that would soon be mourning a World Series loss to the Mets. This was the series with Bill Buckner's infamous gaffe in Game 6, leading to Game 7 in which the Mets won. You could feel that winter was around the corner and it was a depressing time in Boston. Having come up well short in Hawaii from where I hoped I'd be, I could relate to Buckner.

I was still juggling my sleeping arrangements, avoiding my mother as much as I could, and living mostly at my grandmother's place. I stayed in her old room. Frankie was living there, too, staying in my aunts' old room across the hall. Things were still awkward, but I was thirty by then. It had been fourteen years since I'd told Frankie never again. I was safe now.

But then, one morning in early November, he came into my room. He touched my bed, and as soon as he did, I awoke. I jumped up immediately, leaping out of the bed before he could even try to get into it.

"What the f--k are you doing?!" I screamed.

"I was...I uh..."

"You f--king a--hole!"

"I guess I came in here by accident..."

"Bullsh--t, you f--king a--hole!" I paced around. I screamed at him some more, calling him every name I could think of.

"Well, look, I miss Ma," he finally said.

"What the f--k's *that* got to do with anything?! I miss Gram, too! So f--king what?"

Frankie continued to try to explain the inexplicable while I rummaged around the room for my pants and shirt and shoes, releasing a stream of obscenities as I did so.

I had to get out. Daylight was breaking by then and I dashed down the stairs and out of the house. I kept going, not even knowing where. Eventually, I came to Carson Beach where I sat down on a bench trying to calm myself. Thoughts pounded in my head. *Do I kill him? Do I f--king kill him?* Easy, I thought to myself. Take it easy. *Easy does it.* I looked out over the water, taking in the early sunshine on what was otherwise a beautiful autumn morning and wondered what was next for me. I had nowhere to go. I had no one to talk to. Soon, I was crying. I thought the secret had been dead and buried. I couldn't stop the tears. I thought of Ma and wished like hell that I could talk to her, that she'd be sober, that she might be able to do something. Could she just help me? Could she just stand up for me one time?

I spent the morning with rising feelings of agitation and rage, and a whole spectrum of other emotions. I repeatedly tried to calm myself down, but I couldn't stop the groundswell. Eventually, I went to my Aunt Helen's place. Growing up, Helen was always the "cool" aunt, the one you could go to if something was bothering you. Of course, for all the reasons that I'd maintained my silence, I'd never gone to her with this. But I knew I needed to talk to someone and I knew I needed to talk to someone soon. I had to take the risk.

At Aunt Helen's, I paced around her living room and told her about Frankie coming into my bedroom that morning. The words flowed, partly because my level of agitation was higher than my level of anxiety about speaking, and partly because I always spoke better when I stood and moved. I was like Robert Redford's character in *Butch Cassidy and the Sundance Kid* who shot his gun better when he moved than when he stood still. But Aunt Helen didn't let me get very far before she turned and ran out the door towards her daughter's house across the street, telling me as she left, "Wait right here...don't move." Shelly was five years younger than me. I stood bewildered in Aunt Helen's living room, wondering why she'd taken off as she had. In a little while, she returned to tell me a story about one night when Shelly was little.

"You see, Walla and I were going out to a sports banquet," she said. Walla played park league football for the Chippewas, a talented, tradition-rich team that represented Southie. "He was to receive an award. We invited Frankie over to babysit, and when he got here Shelly threw a fit. I mean, she went into hysterics. 'Don't leave me! Don't leave me!' she kept screaming. I'd never seen her like that. I couldn't understand what was going on and she never told me. But I couldn't go. I couldn't leave her. We stayed home. Walla was mad and we fought about it, but I knew we couldn't leave Shelly alone that night with Frankie. That's why I ran over there just now. Sorry about that, Tiny. But I had to know. I had to ask her if Frankie had ever touched her."

"And?"

"She said no."

I nodded as though I believed what Shelly had told her mother. I didn't know if Frankie had touched Shelly, but I knew how difficult it had been for me to even think about mentioning Frankie's assaults on me. In fact, I didn't go into any more details with my aunt that day than the fact that Frankie had tried to get into my bed that morning. Would Shelly have told her mother the truth? Kathy would tell me years later that she was fairly certain Frankie had gotten to most of our cousins. At any rate, Aunt Helen seemed satisfied that Frankie had left her daughter alone. And yet, I couldn't help but wonder if there was more to it than just that one night years ago with the sports banquet. Would that one night alone have been enough to provoke Helen to make that beeline for Shelly's place?

Aunt Helen told me to watch myself around Frankie and to let her know if he tried anything else. She needn't have worried. I wasn't going anywhere near Frankie. For a short while, I bounced around between my mother's place and friends' houses. But I knew getting out of my grandmother's house wasn't enough. I had to get out of Boston, and *now*. Frankie's attempt to get into my bed brought everything racing back to the surface. The secret—the thing I'd been trying to forget for most of my life—was now right in front of my face. And there wasn't anybody to help. That was a fact.

I needed to go away.

I called my friend Jack, whom I had worked with at Kelly's Seafood House in Miami. We'd kept in touch. Since then, he'd gone to California to run a Bennigan's but was now back in Florida, working in Naples. I didn't know exactly where Naples was, but Florida seemed far enough away. Jack worked at the Naples Beach Hotel, and I asked if there might be any jobs available. "Sure," he said, "I can get you a job. And a place to stay. My roommate's moving out. You can live here with me." It was all I needed to hear.

I told everybody a couple of weeks later on Thanksgiving Day at Aunt Helen's house. Since Gram had passed, Helen had taken over the holidays, and everyone was there, Frankie included. I mentioned something about the weather and about how much I'd liked Florida when I'd been down there before. Mostly, I just said things that I figured wouldn't provoke too many follow-up questions that would require further talking on my part—or else that would cause me to explode. At least Helen knew why. That would have to be enough.

The hardest part of leaving was saying goodbye to Matthew and Michael. Matthew was seven and Michael was five. I'd grown so attached to the boys that I cried breaking the news to Matty as we walked over the overpass on Dorchester Avenue to Kathy's house one day. I knew they loved me and I loved them, and I knew they didn't understand my leaving. Of course, I couldn't tell them the real reasons. I needed some excuse that would explain the urgency to leave, and so I told Matty that it had something to do with losing money gambling. "Don't ever gamble," I told him. Mostly, I just tried to assure both boys that my leaving had nothing to do with them. "I just have to go," I said. "I just have to go." They were wonderful boys. I could not have known then what was in store for them, nor could I have known how much they would ultimately resent me for leaving them behind.

Other than Matthew and Michael, who were always welcome to come see me, there was nothing keeping me in Boston this time around and nothing keeping me from Florida. Even Matthew and Michael could have kept me in Boston only temporarily. I had to get out, it seemed to me, to save my life. Naples, where nobody knew me but Jack, who knew nothing of my secret, seemed like just the place for a new start. That Thanksgiving weekend, my friend Ray and I packed up my green Chevy van. Then I said a lot of prayers and started driving south.

# CHAPTER TWELVE
# **FATHER**

The thought of suicide is a great consolation:
by means of it gets one through many a dark night.

– Friedrich Nietzsche –

Jack was renting a condo in the Royal Harbor area of Naples. I moved in with him, and shortly afterward he helped me get a job at the Naples Beach Hotel and Golf Club. I worked as a room-service waiter, worked the bar in the hotel's ballroom, and sometimes worked the hot dog stand that sat between the ninth and tenth holes of the golf course. I purposely took jobs that required interaction with others. I wanted to keep working to improve my fluency of speech. I needed to overcome my stuttering, and I knew of no better way than by putting myself in positions that forced me to talk.

But after a few months of living in Naples and visiting various bars and restaurants around the area, I left the Naples Beach Hotel. I had discovered The Dock at Crayton Cove, a casual, indoor/outdoor water-front restaurant where the wait staff wore shorts. For me—coming to Florida from Boston as the winter was setting in—being able to work outside in shorts as a waiter meant that The Dock had everything I wanted.

And it had more. Most of the people were fun to work with, and I made a lot of good friends. We joked with each other and would hang out together after hours. I still had my stutter, but that didn't seem to matter to anyone, not even me. I even developed the ability to laugh about it. One afternoon, I walked in to the wait staff meeting before my shift to find everyone looking my way and smiling as if they were all in on a secret. I turned to a good friend of mine named Alfie and said, "Alfie, what's going on?"

"Think you might want to check the special board, Fran," he grinned.

I looked at the board advertising that night's special: *Sautéed seafood spinach soufflé with a saffron sauce.*

S's, T's, and F's were the most fear-inducing letters for me to start sentences with. For those letters, "fear" for me stood for F--k Everything And Run. Introducing myself as F-f-f-f-ran or T-t-t-tiny could be a disaster. ("F--k you," on the other hand, seemed to roll right off my tongue. Go figure.) Sautéed seafood spinach soufflé with a saffron sauce? This was inhuman.

"Are you k-k-kidding me?!" I said. The kitchen broke up and I managed to laugh, too, despite the sudden rush of fear that came over me. After all, it was another opportunity to push through. I'll face it, I thought. Besides, it's my job. By then, I'd discovered a few tricks to help ease into fluency with my stutter. Approaching a table quietly and soft-spoken often helped. Delivering food at one table and then turning right away to greet a new party at another table frequently helped with my flow of speech. Sometimes I'd use a physical movement, like bringing water to the table, to help me start a difficult word.

But even with all the tricks, sautéed seafood spinach soufflé with a saffron sauce was an uphill climb for a stutterer like me. At one point the restaurant was really hopping, and I approached my next table to see eight guests. One of them, in a louder than normal voice to catch my attention, asked about the special he saw on the board while walking in. I froze. A thousand thoughts ran through my head. Not one of them was the night's special. My palms began to sweat. My mouth dried up. Eight people were looking at me. It felt as if it was the whole restaurant. They all wore expectant faces as if to say, "Well? The special? You do know what the house special is tonight, yes? You do work here, don't you?" I opened my mouth to say something, but nothing came out. I could feel a bead of sweat slide down the back of my neck.

"Fran," came a warm voice from behind me. One of the waitresses tapped me gently on the back. "Not sure if you noticed, but tonight's special has changed," she continued, looking now at the guests. "The special is sautéed seafood spinach soufflé with a saffron sauce." Help had arrived just when I'd needed it. The special hadn't changed, of course, but the patrons didn't know that. The waitress and my fellow wait staff and bartenders had been keeping a tentative and caring eye on me the whole time. With a little help from my fellow waiters and waitresses that night, I managed to make it through the evening.

I would often spend after-hours and my off days with members of the staff. In fact, the staff of several of the bars and restaurants around town would often hang out together. We were a close-knit community of people more or less around the same age, all involved in the same occupation. We'd go from restaurant to restaurant, drinking at each bar, occasionally for free but always leaving a generous tip for the bartender.

Although I'd been all too keen on leaving Boston after that previous Thanksgiving, I often missed home. Sometimes terribly. Out of nowhere, a warm memory might float into my head—the stickball games, the music, the beach, the Sox and Bruins, the Boys Club, Cape Cod, Nantucket, the Vineyard. And always my friends. One time, I flashed back to sitting on Carson Beach with Johnny Leonard, the two of us drinking beer and singing Beatles songs to the waves as though the ocean was our audience.

Then again, in the winter months, sometimes after taking a run in the balmy and tranquil Florida evening, I might come back to the condo and flip on CNN to see that New England was getting hit with yet another snowstorm. Maybe I didn't miss Boston all that much, after all. Truthfully, because of the memories of abuse, because of the guilt and shame that had followed me out of Boston, I could not make peace with the city of my childhood. It represented more than I was capable of handling. Maybe, someday, I could go back and visit all the old places again and think of them in fondness. But not yet.

Behind The Dock was a restaurant called Marker 4, a nicer, dressier place. I met one of the waitresses who worked there and we began to date. Debra and I weren't terribly serious about each other, but we got along well and had fun together. Eventually, she called it off and began dating another guy. Soon enough, I began dating another girl, Kelly. But a couple of months after we'd last been together, Debra knocked on my door one night at 2:00 a.m. "I have to talk to you, Fran," she said. It wasn't a good time. Kelly was visiting my place, and so we agreed to meet a couple of nights later in a parking lot in Bonita Springs, where Debra told me she was pregnant. She'd done the math and it was mine.

I had mixed feelings. I had always wanted to be a dad, but I imagined different circumstances: married to, and in love with, the baby's mother. But it was important for me to do what was right, and if it meant doing the right thing with Debra, I was happy and willing to try. So was she. She wanted to keep the baby and I wanted to be there for the baby and for Debra. And I wanted to be a dad. We thought we could make it work. Maybe we weren't in love with each other, but we respected each other, and together we hoped we could provide a home for our child. We could be a family. We moved in together, and on June 27, 1989, Sam was born—a healthy, beautiful boy.

I loved being a father. Sam was a treasure and I cherished every minute with him, taking tons of pictures. Debra and I got along, at least at first. Later that summer, the three of us would travel to New York. I'd won a department store contest for amateur athletes. *Sports Illustrated* was coming out with a new line of "Activewear" clothing and several other amateur athletes and I were chosen to model it. We were flown to New York to take in a Mets game at Shea Stadium and be photographed by *S.I.* A full-page advertisement would make it into two issues, one in late November and one in early December. It was a group shot of eight of us amateurs from different sports. I could be seen kneeling and resting my arm on a bicycle wheel. I was smiling. Anybody looking at it would see a good-looking athletic man dressed in fashionable training clothes who appeared as though he didn't have a care in the world. No hidden secrets with that guy. Everything A-OK. Nobody could look at that advertisement and imagine that, only a year and a half later, something inside that man would snap and almost kill him.

In the meantime, being a father made me think of my own father. One night, late after work, about a year after Sam was born, I was drinking with a couple of friends of mine, Dave and Wild Bill. We were in Wild Bill's place, which was just a floor below ours, and somehow the conversation turned to dads. Like me, they didn't really have their dads in their lives either. I didn't say much; I just listened and then excused myself and went upstairs. I had my father's phone number in Vancouver. Kathy had given it to me. I called him. He picked up. We said hello and I invited him to Naples. "What's wrong?" he said. I told him about Sam and that I'd like him to come visit. I said that maybe he'd like to meet his grandson.

"Why? What's wrong?" he said again.

"Nothing's wrong. It's just that you have a grandson here and maybe you can come down and see him."

"What's this all about?" he said. "Are you sure nothing's wrong?"

"No, nothing is wrong! It's just what I said. Look, I never knew you, but maybe Sam can get to know you. I never had you in my life, but maybe you can be a grandfather to my boy."

Almost thirty years later, I still can't believe he came down. Since then, I'd learn that he had visited Southie at times when I was there without bothering to try to see me. But for some reason, in August of 1990, my father came down to Florida and spent five days with Sam and me. A couple of nights my dad and I went out drinking together. One night, we went to see blues singer Luther Kent at a restaurant and jazz club called Tokyo's. It was funny watching my father. I saw some of my own mannerisms. And it was good being with him. I suppose there was a hole in my life that I thought he could still fill. Maybe a relationship with my father would help finally bury the secret. Even better, Sam could have a grandpa.

My father left after that week, and I felt as though we'd kindled a relationship. I sent him pictures of Sam from time to time for a couple of years. He never wrote back. I'm sure he was busy with his life in Vancouver, as I was busy with mine in Naples. Years went by. I would later learn that on a few occasions, he'd come as close to Florida as Atlanta, but he never got in touch with me. If there was ever a chance to form a bond with my father, it was surely lost. That visit in 1990 would be the last time we would ever see each other.

# CHAPTER THIRTEEN
# IN THE MASTER'S HAND

A nation reveals itself not only by the men it produces
but also by the men it honors, the men it remembers.

– JOHN F. KENNEDY, SPEECH IN PRAISE OF ROBERT FROST, 1963 –

On March 15 of 1991, I was planning for "Sam's Second Annual St. Patrick's Day Bash." The previous year's St. Patrick's Day had been Sam's first, and it was my full intention to raise him in the proper spirit of his Irish heritage. To mark the occasion, I'd had a bunch of friends over and even had airbrushed t-shirts of Sam, with his one tooth and wearing a bowler hat. It had been a great time, enjoyed by all.

It would be a little different this year, though. By '91, Debra had moved on. Back in October, I had helped her move into a place close to where her parents were buying a home. They were moving down from Michigan. Debra and I living together just hadn't worked out. There was mutual love for Sam but not enough love between the two of us to make it work.

I figured the St. Paddy's Bash would be good for me. I'd been frustrated. I was still recovering from a knee injury, and I wasn't bouncing back like I'd hoped I would, and certainly not like I'd expected to. Just like when I had jumped back into training after the cycling accident in 1985, I longed for that sense of familiarity again. In fact, I needed it even more now. I had a nagging feeling that as a single, working dad there were only going to be so many more opportunities to race again and that every triathlon I missed would be an opportunity I'd never get back. And besides, I liked training and racing. I liked the competition, camaraderie, and fellowship. Now everything suddenly seemed like an uphill climb.

But I was even more frustrated than I consciously knew. I was tired—tired of putting up a front, of pretending, of acting as if everything in my life was okay. I was tired of trying *so hard*. No matter what I did, the inside was not matching up with how I was presenting myself on the outside. Of course it went well beyond the exercising. It went well beyond the knee injury. There was something deep down that I could not contain any longer. Something that I knew on some level I had to deal with one way or another. My frustration had been building for a while, even before the injury. Way before. My frustration had been building since the age of four, since that first night in the cellar back on O'Callaghan Way.

That's the reason I ran from the cop that night of March 15, 1991 in the parking lot of First Watch and why I took off for the beach, wanting to leap into the Gulf of Mexico to swim away. Far away. I ran, one last time, trying to get away from the nightmares of my life, trying to hang on to denial, refusing to surrender, refusing any kind of acceptance of what had happened in my life. And I was going to fight until the bitter end.

And that's the reason—in the heat of that moment—I'd had those three clarifying thoughts. First, the cop could shoot me (*"which would be all right"*). Second, if the cop let me live, I had to deal with the sexual abuse I'd been trying all my life to run from. I could no longer pretend everything was all right. Third, I couldn't stop running from the cop because it was far too late to explain that epiphany to him.

That last one took the lion's share of my adrenaline, and I kept running until I stumbled enough times for the cop to catch up. My knee finally buckled, just like my life was buckling. But as clear as those clarifying thoughts had been, when the officer jumped on me, the only thing that kicked in was an animal-like instinct of survival. It was a feeling of being assaulted on a primal level. I lost it. I kicked, screamed, punched, and gouged until another officer came along to help calm down the raging man that was me. Looking back, I wasn't fighting the cop. I was fighting for my own life, the entire history of the secret I'd tried so f--king hard to push down, hide, stuff, and cover up.

Now the fighting and the running were over.

I called Debra from jail and she contacted her bosses at the restaurant where she'd been waitressing. They were good enough to post my bail. There would be no St. Patrick's Day Bash that year.

In fact, on St. Patrick's Day, two days later, my name was in the *Naples Daily News* "Police Beat." I went from the anticipation of celebration to the reality of five paragraphs detailing the blow-by-blow from the police report, including these words: "Francis Joseph Fidler was charged with resisting arrest and battery on law officers." It didn't take long for word to get around town. I went into The Dock that day, where I was still frequently hanging out even though I hadn't worked there for a couple of years. The Dock is where everybody hung out, and I knew the day's partying would either begin or end there. Terry, one of the bartenders, saw me as I entered and he lowered his eyes and shook his head. He was one of many to register their disappointment. People asked about Friday night, wondering what the hell happened and what I'd possibly been thinking. I didn't know what to say, really. As clear as those thoughts had been that night, I still wasn't clear on where to go next or even how to begin. No doubt, I had to deal with the sexual abuse; that's all I knew. But I sure couldn't tell that to anybody asking about Friday night's events.

But I also knew that the hiding was over. As embarrassing as the Police Beat article was, and as ashamed and disappointed in myself as I was to have been arrested, I felt a sense of surrender, and in that word, I discovered a flicker of hope.

As for the adjudication of the case against me, I happened to know the assistant D.A. He drank at The Dock, and in fact, he'd moonlighted at Pippins, another restaurant where I worked. He talked to me as a friend and I assumed he'd treat me like one. Consequently, I pleaded guilty to the charges of loitering and prowling, resisting without violence, and battery on a law enforcement officer. In exchange, the battery charge, a third-degree felony, was dropped to a misdemeanor. But my acquaintance was a young, up-and-coming prosecutor, and even as the charge was reduced, he went after me aggressively. I ended up having to serve four degrading weekends in jail and eighty hours of community service, which I completed at the YMCA. Of course, this was all in addition to court costs and attorney's fees. If I thought I was in dire financial straits before, now I certainly was. There would be no more triathlons. Not for awhile.

In addition, I had to be interviewed by a court-appointed psychologist. Tom asked me a slew of questions about my state of mind, and I gave him what I was certain were all the right answers. But as we finished, he surprised me by stating flatly, "I'm going to recommend anger management for you." Part of me struggled like hell at that moment not to prove him right. I seethed underneath, wanting to shout profanities at him and ask him who the f--k he was that he thought I needed anger management! If he knew what I'd been through, he'd be angry, too. It was the same anger I'd kept under control whenever I had thoughts of Frankie, making me feel as though I was about to jump out of my skin. But another part of me was dumbfounded that Tom could see through me so easily, that he could see through the bulls--t, the pretense and distorted pride. That he could see the underlying pain. That he could see that I needed help and didn't know how to ask for it.

For my part, with or without anger management, I knew that to deal with the sexual abuse, I needed to stop drinking. I needed a clear head. I didn't know where to start with the sexual abuse recovery, but

I knew I needed to be sober to figure it out. My big fear with drinking now was that even if I finally started dealing with the abuse, it might keep me from finishing. I'd get part of the way there—to a point where I'd be *comfortable,* before too much pain and anger would surface. Then, figuring that that would be enough, that I would now be okay, I'd quit. And so, as much as I dreaded going through whatever pain or discomfort was in store, I had to stop drinking. Completely. That was priority one.

Initially, when I first started thinking about going to Alcoholics Anonymous, the hope was that doing so would show the judge at my sentencing that I was committed to becoming a better citizen. I'd heard judges would look more favorably upon you if you joined AA. But through time, it would become a lot more than that.

I delayed, of course. I went to the central office one day where they were holding a noon meeting. I stood outside the room and watched people going in, greeting each other. Nobody said anything to me. I leafed through some literature, acting nonchalant, trying to pretend that I was already a member, the chameleon, trying to fit in as always. Of course, nobody recognized me, but that was the idea. I wouldn't have to speak to anybody. And yet, I suppose what I really needed was for somebody to step up and say, hi, are you new? When nobody did, I felt justified in thinking, *screw this; these people aren't friendly.* I turned and left just as the doors to the room were being closed.

I wasn't ready. But a regular breakfast customer at First Watch named Artie had heard about my arrest. Artie was probably twenty years older than me, and he always sat at a table with a group of friends of his. Waiting on them, I'd gotten to know them over time. Artie, Jonesy, Mike, Bruce, Charlie, Jim, and another Charlie. They'd all read the Police Beat report in the paper. One morning, Artie turned to me and said, "You know, Fran, if you think you might have a drinking problem and you need some help, let me know. I'm in AA. If you don't, no worries. Just wanted to mention it." That was all Artie said. No pressure, no obligations.

I thanked him and said I'd keep it in mind. But I still held off. A childhood friend of mine named Tom was planning to visit from Southie. I knew we'd be drinking. I figured I'd stop after Tom went back home. One last hurrah. Tom came and we had a good time. We drank. But as Tom left for Boston, I told him I was going into AA. I had told him about the arrest. "And now there are some things I need to deal with," I said. Tom said he probably ought to do the same, but he also said that he knew that he wouldn't.

Later, having maintained my sobriety, I would find myself feeling an odd sort of survivor's guilt whenever I would think of people I knew who chose not to limit or stop their drinking, and there were a lot of them. Like Ma. Like Bob, a member of an alcohol abuse class I would join. I made friends with him, but he dropped out of the class and started drinking again. The instructor told me that just a couple weeks afterward, Bob lost an arm while operating some machinery on his farm. He'd been drinking.

After Tom went home, I approached Artie. I told him I was ready to attend a meeting. That's the beauty of AA. Attending a meeting, in and of itself, is understood as a request for help. You can make it without ever having to verbally ask for it, something I so obviously had trouble doing. My first AA meeting was Monday, April 22, 1991. I cried during the meeting. I cried during most of the meetings for the first several weeks. I cried for the years I'd wasted running. I cried from anger at myself for never being able to ask for help. But my secret was going to be out now, and I cried in relief, knowing that now I was doing something, that there was something that could be done and I was doing it, starting with not drinking.

On April 25, there was an AA speaker meeting. It was "anniversary night," where members pick up their sobriety chips—tokens that mark the time spent sober, whether it's twenty-four hours or forty-plus years. The meeting was held in a local church, and there were maybe two or three hundred of us. A gentleman by the name of Jim K. got up and shared his story. As he closed, he read a poem called "The Touch of the

Master's Hand" by Myra Brooks Welch. It was a poem about a battered and scarred violin that was being auctioned off. The violin receives no greater than a three-dollar bid until a gray, bearded man comes forward from the back of the crowd and plays a melody "as sweet as the angels sing." The auctioneer starts the bidding again and the bids increase until the violin is sold for three *thousand* dollars. "What changed its worth?" the poem asks. "The touch of the master's hand."

> "...the Master comes,
> And the foolish crowd never can quite understand,
> The worth of a soul and the change that is wrought
> By the touch of the master's hand."

To this day, I consider April 25 as my start in AA. The poem overwhelmed me. I was battered and scarred, but I knew at that moment that a greater force was at work—on me and in me. I was in the Master's hand. And, for the first time in my life, I truly believed I'd be okay.

# CHAPTER FOURTEEN
# COMMITMENT

As long as we are persistent in our pursuit
of our deepest destiny, we will continue to grow.
We cannot choose the day or time when we will fully bloom.
It happens in its own time.

– DENIS WAITLEY –

Jim K. was celebrating thirteen years of sobriety on that evening when he read "The Touch of the Master's Hand." I approached him afterwardand told him how much I loved the poem. It had really touched my heart, giving me a true sense that I was where I needed to be.

"How long have you been coming?" Jim asked.

"Just started," I replied. "But I feel as though I've been through so much just getting here. I felt so much emotion, with the poem you read, that I feel like I deserve ten years."

"Well, if you keep coming back, and you take things one day at a time, and you don't drink in between meetings, you'll get your ten years." For a guy who wasn't used to thinking long-term, a guy who, in fact, had never planned to live beyond twenty-eight, this seemed like a pretty tall order. But after the poem, I felt a connection with the fellowship right away.

The meetings of Alcoholics Anonymous no doubt mean different things to different members. For me, besides the fellowship, which was essential, the idea that stuck with me from the beginning was the organization's philosophy of valuing experience. My past, painful as it was, could not be glossed over, stuffed away, hidden, or forgotten if I was to move forward in life. This was the mistake I'd made all along—running from it, whitewashing it, keeping it secret, keeping my silence. In its proper context, as I was beginning to learn, the alcoholic's past can become a principal asset in letting go and trusting God.

In addition to meetings, I was ordered by the courts to go to six months of weekly alcohol abuse classes. This is where I met Bob, the man who would go on to lose his arm. The classes were Saturday mornings, and they were run by a man named Jim. I liked Jim. He was from Pittsburgh, and we'd often talk baseball. I also had to take Antabuse, a drug that makes you sick if you drink alcohol. I took the Antabuse and got sick even without drinking. Moreover, I'd always had an unnatural fear of becoming addicted to drugs, not that I hadn't tried a drug or two (or three) in the past to help quiet the inner demons. For the Antabuse requirement, I was accountable to Jim, and I asked him if there was anything I could do to not have to take the pills, promising him of course that I wouldn't drink. Jim sensed my sincerity. He knew I was attending meetings daily. He trusted me and released me from the requirement. Better still, he ultimately trusted me enough to release me from the class after only three months. I knew Jim was taking a chance, and his trust in me was more valuable to me than he could have known. I needed this trust. I needed somebody to see in me what I desperately wanted to believe was there: the realistic potential to do the work and turn my life around, to grow up, not drink, be a good father, and give myself a chance to succeed.

I eventually became ready to talk about the sexual abuse. I never discussed it in my early AA meetings, but I'd mentioned it privately to a few of the members, and the David Lawrence Center was suggested to me as a place where I might find outside help. The Center was a local mental health facility where I could engage in one-on-one counseling. I met with a therapist named Chuck, whom I would continue to see once a week for several months. It was tremendously helpful. I finally started talking about the abuse, both Frankie's abuse and my mother's abuse. It was emotionally draining, but I gained energy as we worked and talked through the ugliness of my childhood. Initially, it was hard for me to trust, hard for me to open up, but little by little I grew to trust Chuck and become comfortable with our sessions. Or, maybe more accurately, I began feeling comfortable with being uncomfortable.

Still, I always surprised myself a little by showing up. I had been hiding it all for so long. I never imagined I'd see the day when I could talk about it, cry about it, begin taking steps toward healing from it and letting it all go. As well, I was surprised Chuck showed up each week. I kept imagining how tough it must be to sit there and experience someone else's pain week after week, let alone offer comfort and direction. Part of me figured it would be okay if Chuck gave up on me. Often, I felt as if God was trying to help the wrong guy anyway. This is a theme that would become prevalent for the next several years. I often felt as if I was beyond reclamation, and if Chuck abandoned me that would prove it. "See, God? I told you I was the wrong guy."

My spirituality wasn't necessarily easy to define. I'd always believed, but my relationship with God was not without its rough spots. I spent time angry at God. I cursed God. I resented God for foisting Frankie upon me. But the imagery I had seen in church of Jesus, nailed to the cross, had never lost its power over me. Why would somebody sacrifice himself like that? For strangers? For me? It was humbling. Just as important, maybe more so, was my first real experience of sensing the presence of God. It didn't come in church. It came on the heels of a cry for help, an unsophisticated prayer by a four-year-old boy in his time of greatest need. Of all the things I've blocked from my mind, I could never forget the feeling I'd had at that moment that I was not alone in my suffering.

Chuck eventually advised me to find a group. "Joining a group of sexual abuse survivors would be enormously helpful for you, Fran," he told me. Needless to say, I chafed against the idea. Sharing my secret in a public forum?

Sharing my fear and guilt and anger and shame? I wasn't prepared to go *that* far. *No f--king way,* I thought.

Meanwhile, I remained committed to the AA meetings. I was working on the "twelve steps," the process at the center of the program. Step one was to admit I was powerless over alcohol, that my life had become unmanageable. Step two was to believe in a power greater than myself, a power that could restore me to "sanity," as it was put. I was on step three, making a conscious decision to turn my life and will over to the higher power, as I understood that power to be.

My level of commitment, determination, and persistence surprised me as much as Chuck's showing up for our counseling sessions every week. Maybe I really was on the road to recovery. Being a dad gave me extra motivation to try and get it right, to *change* the dysfunctional cycle before me. I prayed over Sam. I knelt at his bedside at night. "Please, God," I would say, "I know he is your son first, but thank you for this opportunity. Help me be a good dad. Please don't let me mess this up." I didn't have a lot. We lived in a small efficiency apartment, renting from Ray and Nancy Lazo, a kind and caring couple that took a chance on a single dad. One Christmas, Sam and I colored a Christmas tree in his coloring book. I cut it out and taped it to our compact refrigerator and that became our tree. It was all I could do. I placed Sam's presents next to it on Christmas Eve.

On my way to recovery or not, something had been gnawing at me, some unfinished business amid all the other unfinished business. For some reason, I started thinking about the cop who'd chased me and arrested me. He could have shot me in the back and killed me that night. He didn't, and I was still alive. For that, I was now feeling grateful, seeing the attitude of gratitude in my life. And also remorseful to think that I put him or anyone in that position in the first place. I checked the police report and learned that the arresting officer's name was Jon Maines. Sometime around Thanksgiving of that same year, I went to the police station and asked if I could see him.

"I don't know if you remember me," I said when he came out into the lobby. "A couple nights before St. Patrick's Day, I ran from you in the parking lot of the First Watch restaurant. I took off for the beach."

"Yeah, I remember you," he said. His voice was flat, maybe even a little gruff. I supposed I couldn't blame him.

"Well, listen, I just wanted to let you know I'm in AA now, attending meetings daily and trying to work some things out. I have a son and I'm really trying to do better. That night...thanks for not shooting me. I'm sorry I ran. Really sorry. I just felt I needed to come here and tell you that."

"Okay. Well. I hope everything works out for you, I really do. Good luck." And then he turned and went back through the secured door and down the hallway. I guess I could not have expected anything more, and it felt good to have told him what I did.

One night at an AA meeting, I saw a man out in the hall whom I had seen and met a time or two before. "Big Jerry" worked at a restaurant and bar called Page One.

"Jerry," I said, "what are you doing here?"

Big Jerry chuckled. "What do you think?"

Turns out Big Jerry had been sober for five years. Seeing him relieved me of at least one concern. Being around alcohol by working at Page One didn't seem to be a problem for Jerry. Of course, working in the restaurant industry, this had worried me. I heard that some people in recovery couldn't be around alcohol at all, but it was nice to know that it was at least possible and that maybe I could do it if I needed to. I would learn through AA to respect the disease, to be vigilant.

Jerry and I talked. We connected. Turned out he was from Jamaica Plain, a neighborhood in Boston not unlike Southie. He asked me what had brought me to AA and I told him about the arrest, the running, the three thoughts that had crossed my mind that night. He asked me what step I was on and who my sponsor was. A "sponsor" is typically a recovering alcoholic who helps another alcoholic, relating to them what it was like, what happened, and what it's like now after going through the steps. The shared experience of alcoholism makes for a valuable connection. A sponsor can be someone you call when you need emotional support or feel threatened by a relapse. I remember being told, "Don't leave before the miracle happens," and, "Don't go into your head alone—it's a dangerous neighborhood." I'd had a couple of temporary sponsors, Artie and Charlie, and members Don and Lloyd helped me quite a bit as well. But after that night, Jerry became my sponsor.

We met at the First Watch one day for breakfast, the site of my arrest. Outside of the restaurant, Jerry asked, "Fran, are you willing to do anything to stay sober?"

"Anything?" I said.

"Anything."

I hesitated. I had attended enough meetings by this time to know what "anything" meant. Thoughts raced through my head. Do I really want to not drink for the rest of my life? Weddings, funerals, birthdays, holidays? Good days, bad days? Rainy days, sunny days? *Not drink?*

"Fran, it's okay," Jerry said. "It's no big deal. You can have your old life back anytime you want." And then he turned and walked toward the restaurant, leaving me standing there.

I let out a yelp. "Wait!" I said, chasing towards him. "Yes, I'll do anything!" I needed Big Jerry. I wanted him to know I was *in*. For his part, he needed to know I was, too. Why would he waste his time with someone who wasn't committed? Admitting to someone else that I was an alcoholic was another surrender, and a big one.

After breakfast, we went back to Jerry's condo. We went into his bedroom. We had talked about the third step, and it was now about me sharing with another human being my decision to turn my will and my life over to the care of God. We knelt on the floor and held hands and recited the Lord's Prayer. And that was that. All Jerry had in his heart and on his mind was helping me come to a decision with step three, to surrender my life to the care and will of God. It was something of a strange moment, but for me at that point, the stranger thing was that somebody was so committed to helping me without wanting anything in return.

As it happens, Jerry was sexually abused as a child, too. He'd been in a group, and it had greatly helped him. I still wasn't interested in revealing my past to a group of strangers, but the thought that I was now friends with a man of similar background, who had five years of recovery and healing, and that there were others like me—entire groups of people recovering who had been sexually abused as children—was eye-opening to me.

I didn't join Jerry's group, but I began to see Barbara, the counselor who ran it. Barbara floated the idea that Frankie might well have been abused himself as a child. "If you don't deal with it," she said, "you can become an abuser, too." That hadn't occurred to me and I found the idea sick and disturbing. Who would have abused Frankie? Was this yet another family secret that had been kept quiet?

Big Jerry, in the meantime, kept encouraging me through the steps. Step four was to make a moral inventory of myself and five was to admit my defects of character. Six was to be entirely ready to have God remove those defects, and seven was to humbly ask God to do so. Eight was to make a list of all those I had harmed and to be willing to make amends. I made my list and gave it to Jerry. I thought of all the people I had hurt in some way. Guys I might have insulted; girls I had tried to manipulate into bed, mostly out of sexual insecurity. I thought the list was thorough. Jerry looked at it and said, "Well, this is a good start, Fran, but it looks a little incomplete. Take a couple more days with it."

I came back two days later with a slightly longer list. "It's still incomplete, Fran," Jerry said. I looked at him blankly. I couldn't imagine whom I'd left off. And how would Jerry know, anyway?

"*You*," Jerry said at last. "Your name's not on here. You need to make amends to Fran Fidler. And you have to forgive him. I want you to put your name at the top of the list, Fran."

Through tears, I promised Big Jerry I would. I knew he was right. But I was still at a point where the shame and guilt were too great. At AA, Don D., one of the members, was chairing the Thursday night "cookie" speaker meeting, so called because of the cookies that were always available for snacks along with the normal coffee and water offered at all the meetings. Don made it my job to pick up the cookies on my way to the meeting, make the coffee, and to make sure the room was set up for the meeting. He gave me the keys to the church where the meeting was to be held. Service work is a big part of recovery. I begged him not to choose me for the job. "Do you really want to trust me to do this?" I asked. "Do you want to trust me with the keys to the church?" I didn't trust myself. I was a liar, a guy with a shameful secret going through life hiding behind a facade. Who was I, really? I couldn't even say with any degree of certainty that I was even going to show up each Thursday. For all Don knew, I might have been inclined to snatch the picture of Saint Paul off the wall and try to sell it. He had no idea who he was dealing with.

Don, having been in AA a few years, saw it differently. "You can do this, Fran. I know you can." Don's trust, just like Jim's trust at the alcohol abuse classes, was powerful. And needed. Ironically, even though I was on the road to recovery, I had rarely felt worse about myself. Sobriety was forcing me to deal with everything. There was no place to hide. No place to run. It was all coming up to the surface now and I could not escape the shame or the guilt. Drinking had pushed it down, way down, but now it was right in my face. The pressure to drink was enormous and there were times when I would attend two or three or sometimes even four meetings a day.

Obviously, I still needed to address the sexual abuse. I was tired of fighting everything and everyone, and tired of fighting myself. I wanted to let go of my anger. I wanted to laugh more. I didn't want to spend the rest of my life feeling resentful, feeling as though I'd been cheated in life in some way by Frankie's abuse or Ma's abuse or by my stuttering. And I didn't want to be haunted by the decisions I'd made trying to keep my secret a secret.

# CHAPTER FIFTEEN
## SIGNS

A sign has no intrinsic value;
it has one simple purpose: to be a sign.

– UNKNOWN –

About that time, I was house sitting for a running friend. Close by was a library, and I visited it one late afternoon looking for books on running. I checked out several, including a book entitled *Many Lives, Many Masters,* which I assumed had something to do with athletes and their various coaches. Instead, when I began to read it, I discovered it was a book about hypnotherapy wherein the author detailed a case study of past-life regression. I was immediately intrigued. Could this really be? Not long after that, I came across the name Sharon Bruckman.

Sharon was the publisher of *Natural Awakenings,* a Naples-based wellness magazine geared towards holistic health. She was also a hypnotist. I called her and set up an appointment. There was so much I didn't know about my early childhood. Could hypnosis help? In our first session, Sharon explained the process. We weren't necessarily going to go back to my childhood, although that might happen. More importantly, we were just going to go wherever I'd be moved spiritually to go.

Off and on for several months, I saw Sharon. One time, we did go back to my early years. This is when I saw myself handcuffed to a downspout in Natick, in the rain, crying for my mother to help and having nobody come for me. In another session, I had a vision of a hand. I was listening and hearing a voice encouraging me to reach out and grab hold. I could see my hand reaching, trying, stretching for the other. Mine was small, like a child's. I imagined it was my hand at around age four. Try as I might, I couldn't reach the other hand, but I knew I needed to. It was hard and I found myself crying, but the voice continued to encourage me to try. *Don't give up. Reach. Stretch. Don't ever give up.* Finally! I reached the hand and I heard the voice telling me I was safe. *This is who you are,* the voice said. *This is who you were always to be. You have always been loved. You have always been protected.* "The Touch of the Master's Hand" came to mind: "... the Master comes and the foolish crowd never can quite understand the worth of a soul and the change that's wrought by the Touch of the Master's Hand."

In another session, I envisioned myself in heaven. I was sitting on a couch and Jesus, my Lord, was asking for somebody to help His children on earth who had been abused. I raised my hand enthusiastically, like a schoolboy with what he believes is the right answer. Jesus, walking back and forth talking, stopped in front of me. "It's going to be hard," He said. "You'll have to be abused yourself and you're not going to remember any of this until you come through it. And lots of people choose never to come through it."

Was this what my abuse was about? Was this the reason for it? I had more questions than answers and had a difficult time believing it all. How could I trust that this was the right path for me? I continued thinking that God had the wrong guy, but a series of life events and *ah-ha!* moments continued to change things for the better—events and moments I could only describe as signs of spiritual guidance.

Within, I was gaining strength and resolve. In 1993, I started working at a local fitness center. I had originally gone to work there part-time, more or less to get a free membership. I worked the front desk but eventually became certified in fitness and health training and started working full time on the floor. I liked it. One day in July of that year, a man by the name of George came into the fitness center, and as we talked about his health and fitness goals I asked him what he did for a living. He said he was a writer. "Really? I always wanted to write," I said. Why I said that, I have no idea. Immediately, I heard my inner voice say, *No you don't.*

George mentioned a writing class that he taught in his home. "You should come to the next one," he said.

"Sure," I said. "Sounds great." *No it doesn't. Why are you lying to this man?*

I would see George for a couple of more months, and he eventually stopped coming to the center. I called him one time to check in on him, and he said his life had become busy again, but he promised to keep in touch. In December, he gave me a call, letting me know that a new writing class of his was starting up in January. He wanted to know if I was interested. "Sure," I said, thinking I'd call him the night before the first class to let him know that something had come up and, as sorry as I was, I just wouldn't be able to attend.

But the night before the class was to meet, I was struck by the idea that I *had* to go to it. Maybe it was my new sense of wanting to be responsible and do what I said I would do. Maybe it was a thought planted by the universe. On some level, however, I still figured going was wrong. I wasn't a writer. What the hell was I thinking? Ultimately, I decided to go to George's class, trusting in the thought that had hit me to go, trusting in the universe. But even with that, I hedged. I figured I'd show up and George would excuse me from the class once he knew that I was only interested in writing about my sexual abuse as a child. If that wasn't enough, he'd discover quickly that I had no idea where to start and had no formal writing skills. At least then, I could say I tried.

"This probably isn't the right class for you, Fran," George would say, and I'd be off the hook. Of course, there was the thought this could be the same hook that all these years I'd been hanging myself with.

There were to be ten people in the class. When I showed up, there was just George and one other student, a woman who happened to be a counselor at a local treatment facility that specialized in recovery for mental health and substance abuse issues through the use of strength and compassion. George talked a little about himself. Much to my surprise, he mentioned he'd been in Alcoholics Anonymous for quite a few years. Then the counselor spoke, and then I spoke. I talked about my interest in writing as a means by which to work through my sexual abuse. George and the other student exchanged glances. Here we go, I thought. My ticket to leave.

George spoke first. "Fran," he said, "I think you're in the right place." The counselor agreed.

The class would be the first step in what would become years of journaling, filling notebook after notebook with every thought that came to mind. George asked me if I'd ever heard of *The Artist's Way*. I told him no, but I'd heard of "My Way," AA's way, the highway, and your way. He ignored my flippant response, went to his bookshelf, and brought over a book by Julia Cameron. *The Artist's Way*, he said, delved deeply into the link between spirituality and creativity, and as he handed the book to me, I felt a strange and strong sense that *I need to get this book*. In the days before Amazon, I went to my local Books-A-Million, then to Barnes & Noble and Borders. No one had *The Artist's Way*. I declined to order it, telling myself I'd go back to the Books-A-Million sometime and order it later. Besides, I told myself to justify my procrastination, if all of this was really God's will, then God would somehow make the book accessible.

I'd been attending different churches around this time, one of which was Unity of Naples, which had a wonderful Irish pastor named Jack. One day I went to the church with Sam to say prayers for my nephew who was, by then, struggling with addiction issues of his own.

Afterward, we went into the church bookstore where I decided to look for books by Thomas Moore. Moore, who had written *Care of the Soul* and *Soul Mates,* as well as other inspirational books, was scheduled to speak at the church. While at the checkout, I casually asked the girl behind the counter if they had a book entitled *The Artist's Way,* figuring, of course, that they wouldn't.

"Yes," she said, her eyes brightening. "We *just* got in six copies. I haven't even had a chance to shelve them yet! They're right behind you on that table there."

*Of course they have it,* I thought. *Of course.*

I returned the books I had come to purchase and bought *The Artist's Way* instead. On my way out, the girl called to me. "Hey, you know, I think somebody's holding a class based on *The Artist's Way.* There's a flier on the door."

*Of course there's a class on it,* I thought. And just then I heard an inner voice reply in kind: *of course.* I asked the girl for a pen and wrote the phone number down from the flier.

By then, it was occurring to me more and more that doors were opening, doors I hadn't seen before but doors that I began to realize had always been there. Maybe I couldn't always anticipate them, but I liked the idea of being ready, of trusting in the process that was in front of me. My new life of prayer, recovery, and sobriety was revealing opportunities for introspection and growth without me even really looking for them. Of course I still needed to do the work, and at times, I still found myself resisting. *Why me? What's so special about me? Are you sure you haven't got the wrong guy?*

But doors kept opening. The class on *The Artist's Way,* for instance, had started two weeks prior. I called the instructor who ran the class anyway—sure that he would tell me it was too late to join—just to prove to God that I was not the man he was apparently intent on making me. But at least the call would show that I tried. I left a voicemail letting the instructor know that if he ever had another class in the future, to keep me in mind. The following day, I had a client cancel, and I happened to be home at a rare time. And that's when the phone rang. It was the instructor. "You're in luck," he said. "We started off slow, so you haven't missed much at all. If you can read up to chapter two, come and join us. We definitely have room for you." I didn't even want to be in one writing class, and now I was in two.

*Of course he has room,* I thought. *Of course.*

In the class, everyone shared briefly why they were there and when it was my turn, I talked about what it was I was trying to work through. A man named Greg approached me afterward. "Something told me to come here tonight," he said. "I had a strong sense that there would be somebody here who could help me. Somebody who would understand what I've been through. I was undecided, but I came. I'm really glad I did." Greg had fifteen years of sobriety and was now ready to let go of the wounds and scars from childhood abuse. Another sign?

Later the following year, there was a conference in New York with Julia Cameron. A girl I was seeing encouraged me to attend. Reading through the brochure, I saw that Brian Weiss was also attending. Weiss was the author of *Many Lives, Many Masters,* the book I'd checked out of the library about past life regression. With him and Cameron both, I simply had to go to the conference. The problem was that I was running the Boston Marathon that year, and I knew I couldn't afford both trips only weeks apart.

I mentioned the conference to a client of mine named Harry, a retired professor from Columbia University in New York. "Where's the conference?" he asked. I told him it was at the Marriott Marquis on Broadway, close to Times Square. "Really? My wife and I have an apartment near there. Just one block off Broadway, up around 99th on the West End. You're more than welcome to use it. I have a bike there. You're welcome to use that, too." Harry barely knew me; he'd been training with me less than three months.

Something similar happened about five months later. This time it was a conference with Brian Weiss in Boston. I had gotten a lot out of the New York conference, and I had hoped to see Weiss in Boston, too. But I put it off for similar reasons as before. This time I was running the Chicago marathon the following month and I couldn't afford both trips. I called my brother Danny in Boston, leaving him a voicemail and floating the idea of staying with him should I decide to make the trip. I mentioned that he could reach me the following day around noon at the home of some friends where I was house sitting. The next day at noon, the phone rang. But it wasn't Danny. It was a local doctor's office asking to speak to Mary Rose Flanagan. It was the wrong number, but I was curious as to how the doctor's office had gotten this particular number. It was a strange hour to be calling, too—lunch hour for the typical office. The woman on the other end said merely that this was the number she'd been given. The real curiosity was this: Mary Flanagan was my mother's married name. What were the odds? After I hung up the phone, I sat there stunned. This, to me, was too much of a coincidence. I made up my mind to go to Boston no matter what.

Typically, I still waited until the last minute, thinking I was crazy to be following what seemed more and more like a whim. I didn't have the money to be flying here and there anyway. I waited until the day before the conference and then asked Debra if she could pick up Sam, telling her I needed to go to Boston for the weekend. Then I got a ride to the airport from my friend Ann. There was a 4:40 p.m. flight, but I knew there was no time left to get a ticket. I even told Ann that. "But it's still important for personal reasons that I try," I explained to her. I sure wasn't going to mention inner voices and wrong phone calls to people with my mother's name.

We got to the airport around 4:30 and I left my bag in the car, figuring I'd be returning from the airport with Ann, knowing I was too late. Surely, the doors of the plane had been closed by then. At the ticket counter—of *Spirit Airlines*—I asked about the Boston flight. "There aren't any available seats, right?"

"Why, yes there are," the smiling man at the counter said. "We have just one more seat available. You'll have to hurry to make it, though."

I ran back to the car, saying to myself, *you've got to be kidding me. Am I really going to go?* I grabbed my bag and, this being pre-9/11, was able to run directly to the gate, making it just in time. As I boarded the plane, I noticed the faces of the passengers and maybe it was my imagination but it seemed to me they all wore the same expression—a look that said, where have you been? We've been waiting for you.

I found my seat. Second row, middle. There was space for my bag in the bin right across the aisle. Then I sat down and took out my yellow pad of paper and began to write.

Of course there was a seat on the plane. Of course.

# CHAPTER SIXTEEN
# SO MUCH TO SAY

Do not pray for easy lives, pray to be stronger men.

– JOHN F. KENNEDY –

In August of 1993, I visited my mother in Boston. She was in the hospital. A lifetime of smoking and drinking was catching up to her. She had emphysema. Her alcoholism had weakened her, and her body was failing. I drove to the hospital one evening, expecting to get there around 8:00 or so, but I ended up making a wrong turn. Foolishly thinking I still knew my way around Boston, even though it had been a good eight years since I'd driven around the city, I decided to take the Mass Turnpike but confused it with Mass Avenue and Storrow Drive. I took an exit for Watertown when I realized my mistake and turned around, doing what I thought was a 180 but what ended up being a 360. Unaware, I kept going in the wrong direction until I saw that damnable sign once again, the one that always seemed to be looming in front of my path: "Entering Natick." *Are you kidding me?* I had surrendered, I thought. What more did I have to do? Why could I not move past Natick and all that it had represented for me?

I stopped the car and said a prayer. Speaking about Natick in general and what it had come to represent, I said *I forgive you. I surrender. I wish to stop fighting—you, myself, anything, or anyone.*

By the time I'd dealt with my emotions, found the right roads, found parking at the hospital and found Ma's room, a thirty-minute journey had taken four hours.

Ma was alert and sitting up in her bed, as though she'd been peacefully waiting for me all along. But she was weak and the color was washed out of her face. It was apparent to me at that moment that she didn't have much time left. I sat beside her and took her hand.

There was so much I wanted to say to her, so much I'd held in over the years. Deep down I was angry, resentful, bitter. I never felt these feelings consciously for any more than moments here and there, but they were always lurking under the surface. I knew that, but I also knew these were the feelings I needed to overcome if I was going to be able to move forward in my life.

I had nothing planned to say. Because of what I'd been apprised about her condition, I hadn't expected to say anything, really. But then I heard myself speaking to her.

"Ma," I said, "I just want you to know that I'm good. Sam's good. I'm in AA and have been for two years. I've been putting my life together. And I want you to know that I forgive you. I believe you did the best you could with what you knew."

She didn't say a word, but tears pooled in her eyes and she gripped my hand a little harder. The next day, I talked to her doctors, whom I discovered had had no idea about her lifetime of drinking. She'd failed to mention that part.

When I returned to Naples, I was grateful for having spoken to Ma. Still, I wished she had chosen to speak to me. I suppose that's why I gave her my understanding, in hopes of hearing her explain herself. I hoped that she might tell me she was sorry, that she'd take some responsibility, that she'd let me know that it was never about me. Maybe she'd talk to me about the bad decisions she had made, and maybe even about the demons she had been fighting her whole life. I had hoped to know what those demons were.

Ma lived a life of self-loathing that she had tried to drink herself away from. Years earlier, at a funeral service at St. Monica's Church, I took communion and brought it back to where Ma was seated, offering it to her. Even then, even before my own recovery, I knew Ma was a tormented and haunted soul and had been for at least as long as I had known her. And I knew she needed to forgive herself. But Ma shook her head when I offered her the communion. It could have been pride, but I had the distinct impression it was more a sense of unworthiness. And I asked her, "If you believe, then what do you think Jesus died for if not for times like this? Please accept His forgiveness for you. It's not a crutch; it's the truth." But she said nothing.

In December of '93, just four months after I had seen her in the hospital, Ma called me one day, telling me she was making a remarkable recovery. "They're going to write about me in a medical journal," she declared. I knew the truth was otherwise. Ma was hearing what she wanted to hear from the doctors and ignoring the stuff she didn't want to hear. "I'll be going home soon," she said.

"Ma, make sure you're ready," I said. "Stay in the hospital as long as you can. There are people there to take care of you and spend time with you. That's the place you should be." Of course, I also knew that at the hospital, Ma had no access to cigarettes or liquor.

Not long afterward, the hospital did release her. I imagine there was nothing more they could do for her. Back in her own home—alone—she started drinking and smoking again. Kathy reported to me that within two weeks of leaving the hospital, Ma's condition was worse than ever. Still, she somehow hung on until September of 1994, when her body and spirit finally gave out. She was sixty-one.

By then, I had finally joined a group of male sexual abuse survivors. I'm still not sure how I scraped up the courage. I think I had come far enough that I wanted to see it through, whatever that entailed. I still had all the anger and frustration to let go of. I thought of Sam. Maybe

I was doing it for him. To be the best father I could be, I needed to be a better man. That meant I needed to unlearn and relearn a lot.

The group was one that Barbara, the counselor for Big Jerry's group, was facilitating. The group met every Monday night and had at most six or eight guys at any one time. Men would come and go. There were three of us who made the classes regularly. Besides me, there was Bob, who made all of the meetings, and Doug, who made most of them. I became good friends with both, especially Bob, who had a wife as well as children close to Sam's age. The group was helpful, to a degree. It was good to know that I was not alone in my feelings, that there were others who felt the shame, hurt, anger, and bitterness that I felt. We used a book by Laura Davis about surviving childhood sexual abuse called *The Courage to Heal Workbook,* which was of great help, resource, and comfort.

In September, I flew up to Boston for my mother's funeral and made a decision to deliver the eulogy. No one else had volunteered to do it, and I knew that Ma deserved at least a few words. Of course I was nervous. "Stuttering Tiny will now be delivering the eulogy," I imagined would be my introduction. "Make yourselves comfortable, folks. We'll be here all day."

But I was uneasy for another reason, too. What would I even say? Kathy and I talked about it in the car from the funeral home to the church and we had a difficult time thinking of a single good thing to say about Ma. Yes, there were those rare memories of going to the beach with her or maybe to a Bruins' game, but at that moment, the good moments were hard to bring to the surface. Madonna's song "This Used to be My Playground" played in my head as we drove through the streets our mother had grown up in, the same streets I had grown up in. Ma had childhood dreams at one time. What happened to them? What happened to her?

At the church, I managed to say some words about Ma's friendships. She had a large group of loyal friends from her childhood and from the many jobs she worked and everybody called her "Pal." "She was good friends with a lot of people," I said. "But," I added, "she should never have been a mother. Still, Kathy and I love her and we're happy she's finally at peace." Then, speaking for our half-siblings, I said that I knew that Georgie, Florence, Jackie, Danny, and Michael were happy she was finally at peace, as well. It was all I could think of to say.

————

The night before the funeral, I was at the viewing at the funeral home. People were milling about, coming in and out, paying their respects. Frankie was there. Needless to say, we didn't have much to say to each other. At one point, he came up to me and asked how Sam was doing. Sam was four at the time. Later, it would strike me that this was the age I was when Frankie had first molested me. "He's fine," I said, and then I drifted away from him. But within a half-hour's time, he approached me twice more, ostensibly to make small talk, but each time asking about Sam. Maybe he just didn't know what else to say to me. His older sister, my mother, had just passed away, after all. But after the fourth time, all in a short period of time, his asking about Sam was more than I could take. I was trying to process my mother's death. I was trying to be quiet and respectful, even hidden. I found myself thinking about the real reason I'd left, and how I'd found AA and the sexual abuse class, in spite of everything that had happened. And now this son of a b--ch was asking about my son. I wanted to grab him by the throat. We were in a funeral home, after all, and the thought hit me fleetingly that it sure would be convenient to send him off in a box to the cemetery with my mother. So much for what I'd been learning about forgiveness and serenity.

My uncles Joe and Larry were there. So was Danny and so was Sean, my best friend and Sam's godfather. I approached each one individually, asking to see them downstairs in the basement of the funeral home. Each went down. And then I told Frankie I needed to talk with him. "Let's go downstairs," I said.

My silence had to end.

I didn't know what I was going to say. I hadn't planned it. I just knew I had to finally get it out in the open. Enough was enough. I had mentioned the abuse to Uncle Joe, Danny, and Sean. When I had been up to Boston the previous August visiting Ma in the hospital, I had told Uncle Joe. I'd watched him turn ghostly white in front of me. I'd felt terrible; I'd hated the thought that I had hurt him, maybe embarrassed him. I don't know why I hadn't told him earlier. Joe had always tried to look out for me, but I guess I hadn't trusted him enough to think he could have helped me with this. I'm not even sure why I finally told him that day, but in those brief moments of risk and trust, he seemed to age right in front of me. We hadn't talked about it since. And now I was about to bring it up again. I hated doing it, but I knew it was the right thing to do.

"Look, this is for me," I started. Then, pointing at Frankie, I said, "This is about you, but you have nothing to say here. Nothing. Right here, right now, I am holding you accountable for all of those times you crawled into my f--king bed."

Frankie tried to say something but Danny gave him a look and he stopped. I continued. "You f--ked up my life. You have made me miserable for a long, long time. You led me to second-guess and doubt myself. In front of these men, I am holding you accountable for crawling into my bed and sexually molesting me from when I was four until I was sixteen. And threatening me, saying that you would tell Ma that I started it, that it was my fault. And you will never ask about Sam again. You will never see him and you will never be in the same room with him."

I finished saying what I had to say and Sean and I went upstairs. Larry and Frankie and Joe followed soon afterward, and then Danny came up shortly after that. Larry said something to Auntie Helen about it, telling her it was the wrong time and place. But I knew better. The moment had been as unplanned and unprepared for as I had been for the moment. But as much as I felt I might have caught everybody blindsided by what I'd shared, and as much as I wanted to apologize to them for confronting Frankie at that particular moment, I knew that as far as my family was concerned, there would never be a right time and place. Nobody was ever supposed to break the precious f--king silence.

# CHAPTER SEVENTEEN
# A PATH FOR ME

Praying for one's attacker is an easier—and much safer—
task than offering unconditional forgiveness and reconciling
with unrepentant abusers. Requiring repentance before
granting forgiveness gives victims another way to protect
themselves while remaining true to the biblical text.

– MARIA MAYO –

Confronting Frankie was cathartic. As much as I hated having to do it, I felt relief. Paradoxically, I also felt more vulnerable. It was a strange mix of feeling insecure yet somehow more grounded. If there were family members who had preferred that I stayed quiet, so be it. I moved quickly past my initial thoughts of *how could they?* Though the thought of any resentment toward me was painful, I decided I'd be okay with it. What Frankie had done—how could anybody have reasonably expected me to continue to remain quiet about it? Even I wondered how I could have remained quiet about it for all those years. Of course I knew the answer. For the longest time, I had so desperately wanted normalcy. I wanted to believe my family was normal, and I wanted to portray that to the outside world. I wanted to believe my childhood was normal. I wanted to believe it in the hopes that the painful memories would disappear along with all of their damaging effects. But of course they never could.

It was hard opening up to Frankie's brothers, to share the secret, but in doing so, I realized I'd cut the pain in half. I didn't have to carry the burden alone any longer. I didn't have to feel alone and isolated in the shame anymore. Maybe they didn't want to hear it, but at least maybe they could understand some of the choices I had made in my life. I felt freedom. I was truly alive—far from perfect but no longer ashamed, in hiding, and feeling like damaged goods. More than anything, I felt a renewed hope. Ever since I'd run from the cop that night, I'd known that I had needed to deal with the childhood sexual abuse. The day had arrived, and although it came not necessarily with any careful planning of my own, I had dealt with it.

I stopped attending the sexual abuse group in October of '94. By this point, the thing that was helping me the most was journaling, what I had started back in George's writing class, something I'd been inspired to do by Julia Cameron's *The Artist's Way*. Cameron's recommendation was to write three pages first thing in the morning. "Morning pages," she called them. They could be about anything— just something to encourage the creative flow of spirit and life. I started out writing gibberish, but soon enough my writings were becoming less arbitrary explorations of everything I'd been through. Even still, for the most part, the writings were all over the place, disjointed and often random in subject matter. But I threw myself into it and the material flowed, even overflowed. The journaling became a very effective piece of my healing. I hoped that if I stuck with it, the writing would help me get through to the other side. After a while, it wasn't so much a case of having to fill up three pages; it was a case of not being able to stop myself from filling up way more than three pages. Somewhere along the line, the idea occurred to me that someday I'd have to organize all of my ramblings into a coherent narrative.

Of course, throughout my life, I had always planned on "someday" doing one thing or another. I saw a page in a magazine once with a picture of an island and the words "Someday Isle" above it. I ripped it out of the magazine and taped it to my bedroom wall as a reminder that I didn't want my "somedays" to be imaginary, unrealizable dreams. I wanted to believe that Someday Isle was a real place, and I thought to myself that *Someday Isle* write a book to share my story and hopefully help others.

In the meantime, I made periodic stops at the police station to see Jon Maines, my arresting officer. Ever since that first time I had stopped in to see him around Thanksgiving in 1991, I felt compelled to let him know somehow that I was serious about turning my life around. I'd suspected that after I'd left that day, he had regarded me as just another hard-luck case who was making promises he couldn't—or wouldn't—keep. And so every other year or so, I dropped by. Most of the times Jon was out, but I'd leave a Thanksgiving Day card or Christmas card, depending on the season, with a couple of notes jotted down. "Hope you are well," I'd write. "Things are good with me. Still in AA. Sam is doing great."

Part of the reason I kept going back might have been my underlying competitive nature. To show Jon, just in case he was skeptical, that I was up to the challenge of bettering myself. I knew I lacked accountability, and I knew I needed it. I was accountable in AA, and I was account-able with Sam. Those were good for my soul. Visiting Jon Maines on occasion was, as well. Part of it was also out of the respect I had for law enforcement, a respect I'd gained through Uncle Larry's service with the Boston Police Department. I felt bad for putting Jon through what I'd put him through that night. And part of it was the hope that maybe—just maybe—I could make a difference in some small way for Jon himself—that perhaps his seeing my progress might help him know that his work had real meaning. I would be more right than I knew.

In 1999, I organized a 10K and 5K run for charity, something I had always wanted to do and something I'd do for the next five years. In that time, we'd have some great runners show up, like Bill Rodgers, Billy Mills, Joan Benoit Samuelson, Ted Corbitt, and other running dignitaries like Dave McGillivray, Roy Benson, and Brian Crawford, to name a few. I also became the Leukemia Team in Training run/walk coach in Naples. For the 2000 runs, the cause was Youth Haven, a charity that worked with abused children. In particular, the money raised would go to Jay's Cottage. Youth Haven operated Janet and Jay's Cottages, emergency shelters for abused girls and boys, respectively. I felt that abused boys weren't getting enough attention and help. I asked Jon if he would be willing to be the official starter of the races. He was honored.

In 2001, I went to the police station and dropped off my ten-year AA medallion chip. I couldn't think of anybody else I'd rather share it with. And then in 2005, I happened to be at Barron Collier High School for a football game, where I was assisting the visiting Naples High team. I spotted Jon talking to the Naples coach. It turned out that Jon's son was entering high school and showed promise in football. Jon and his wife were trying to determine where he should play.

I walked up and said hello, and Jon and I began talking. Then he introduced me to his wife Kathy. "So *this* is Fran," she smiled. Jon had told her about me. Kathy then encouraged Jon to relate a story. In 2001, he was working an internal investigation. Apparently there was a bad cop on the force. The experience had left Jon weary and cynical. It's a point I imagine all police officers face at one time or another. Sooner or later, the day-to-day dealings with society's worst drag you down, more so if the criminal you happen to be investigating is one of your own. Jon returned to the station at the end of one long day during the investigation, wondering why he was even on the police force, wondering if it was worth it, wondering if he was even making a difference. That happened to be the day I had dropped off my ten-year chip. Jon had his answer. Jon had made a difference.

In 2007, I met a woman. It was during the Sunrise to Sunset Relay, stretching 170 miles. Teams of seven to twelve runners raced from the picturesque setting of Jensen Beach Causeway Park on the Atlantic

Coast to the beautiful Edison and Ford Winter Estates in Fort Myers on the Gulf Coast.

Gina had been living with an active alcoholic, and after leaving him, her main hope was that someday she might meet a man who didn't drink and who regularly attended church. I guess I came along at the right time. Gina got a feel for how serious I was about my triathlon training when I rode my bike one afternoon from Naples to where she worked on Sanibel Island, a distance of forty miles. "You rode all the way here?" she asked. "On your *bike?*"

We dated for close to eight months before I felt comfortable mentioning to her my childhood history of sexual abuse. There was a silence and then she said, "Me, too." Gina's abuse was also at the hands of a prominent family member. Like mine, it started when she was around four, but her first clear memories were from around the age of eight. The abuse continued until her sophomore year of high school when, with the encouragement of an understanding boyfriend, she did something I didn't have the courage to do: she told somebody about it; namely, her health teacher. Her abuser was confronted, and he confessed. He did a few days in jail and then there was counseling for the family, including a forced apology from the abuser, which not surprisingly, meant little to Gina. Neither did the counseling. Gina and her abuser remained estranged for the rest of his life.

Gina went through life feeling all the same things I felt: guilt, shame, insecurity, mistrust. We understood each other almost instinctively, and I can't help but wonder if some of that understanding was present between us even before we knew about each other's pasts. Was this the reason we were drawn towards each other?

Gina and I were married in October of 2008. Don, the man who had trusted me with the keys to the church back when I had started in AA, set up a chapel on the beach. Julie and Hank, personal training clients who had become friends, opened their home to us and bought the cake. The wedding was small but well attended by fitness buddies and friends from AA.

In 2011, I received my twenty-year AA chip. Presenting it to me was none other than Jim K., the man who had read "The Touch of the Master's Hand" at one of my first meetings, twenty years prior. I'd been so moved by the poem and by all that had happened to me in such a short period of time that I had told Jim that night I thought I'd already earned my ten-year chip. "Well, if you keep coming back," he'd said, "and you take things one day at a time, you'll get your ten years." Now I had twenty.

One year later—twenty-one years after that desperate run through the parking lot of First Watch, across the street and into the park, thoughts of life and death running through my head—my twenty-one-year chip was presented to me by the man who tackled me that night. By then, Jon and I had become good friends. So had Kathy and Gina. We attend the same church, and we've remained good friends.

Life is good today. Sam has now graduated from law school in Boston and passed his bar exam. I don't have the words to describe how proud I am of him. I'm grateful that I could be there for him, that I haven't picked up a drink during all this time, and that Sam had the parental influence I had been so wanting in my own childhood. Not perfect, but sober. I wish he had loving grandparents to witness this beautiful time in his life of accomplishment and celebration, and if I continue to harbor any resentment at all towards my mother, it's that she could not be there for her grandson. I remember one trip to Boston in particular when Sam was an infant and we stayed with Kathy and visited Ma. Ma was drunk when we showed up and I thought, *you couldn't even stay sober to see your grandson?*

As for me, I still take things one day at a time. I think that's all any of us can do. In my triathlon training, I became intimately familiar with the concept of "the wall." You hear about it especially with marathon running. Somewhere around twenty miles into the twenty-six point two-mile race, you find yourself hit with a wave of fatigue and loss of energy, caused by a depletion of glycogen in the liver and muscles. Your body is telling you to stop. It's a phenomenon common to any endurance sport athlete and it's an overwhelming feeling. Serious athletes train for it. You train for longer and longer distances, little by little postponing the point at which you might hit the wall. Each time you go a little farther until you can go the distance. There are setbacks, and you might crash and burn a few times along the way, but, in time, you train your body to finish the race. You come through the other side. You break through the wall. I have come through the other side—through prayer, hard work, consistency, luck, good fortune, and, most conspicuously looking back, through the hand of God.

I have broken through *my wall.*

Along the way, though I couldn't always see it at the time, the universe was making, and continues to encourage me to follow, a path less traveled. That much now seems clear. That much I am listening to.

The business that remained unfinished was the gathering up of all my notes and journals to attempt to put everything into a coherent narrative. I hoped my story might help somebody suffering through their own form of hell, whether related to childhood sexual abuse, addiction, or whatever it might be. And I hoped to shed some light on the pervasive nature of sexual abuse. Your neighbor might be a victim. Your co-worker or your fellow student. Your cousin. Even your sister or brother. The silence is pervasive, too.

I also hoped the memoir might bring a little closure, might help me finally make sense of my twisted childhood. But where to start? Eventually, I decided to begin with the beginning. The *real* beginning. I started with a cop yelling "Stop!" in a restaurant parking lot two days before St. Patrick's Day, 1991.

# EPILOGUE

*God is great; I am not.*

You never get over sexual abuse. You can never get to the point where it's no longer a part of you. It will always be a part of you.

You can get past it, however. You can break through the wall.

That's what I have learned.

At least for me, a lot of getting past it required forgiveness. What does it mean to forgive your abuser? I forgave my mother to her face as she lay in her hospital bed. There would be no such face-to-face forgiveness for Frankie. There never will be. But I knew that at some point, I needed to let go of the hate and the anger I felt for him. I'm not above admitting that there were moments—fleeting, I am happy to say—when I fantasized about reaching out to people I knew who had connections with people who would be more than happy to inflict pain on Frankie. But I know that revenge opens wounds; it doesn't close them. Fall down that rabbit hole and you might never get out.

Eventually, I knew I needed to forgive Frankie so that the abuse and the decades-long after-effects would stop controlling me. Revenge and hatred meant I was still being controlled. Forgiveness meant freedom. And I didn't want to wait any longer. I needed to find a healthy path and I needed to stay on it. And so I forgave Frankie. Not in person, for what would that accomplish? My mother never asked for forgiveness, but I knew that on some level, even if she felt undeserving of it, she must have craved it. Frankie never asked for forgiveness, and I could never imagine him having any desire for it, or even feeling as though it was necessary. And so delivering it was never a consideration. I forgave him, but I forgave him for my own sake. Even still, I find myself having to work at it. My forgiveness is a continuous work in progress.

Of course Frankie was not the only person in this drama I needed to forgive. I needed to forgive myself as well. To this day, I sometimes feel, and accept, shame and guilt. Not for the "secret" that I carried with me all those years, for I now understand the power dynamics of childhood sexual abuse. I can't feel guilt for being a victim. But I sometimes feel guilt and shame for keeping quiet about it. For not finding my voice earlier. What if Frankie had molested others after me? Knowing the pattern of sexual predators, that seems more than possible. What if my speaking out would have prevented that?

Why was my shame so deep, and why did I keep quiet for so long? I prayed to overcome it, to be strong, to be tough enough, to move on past it. I tried to pretend, of course, that nothing was wrong. Denial, my major strategy for years, required that I stay silent. But there was also the unstated obligation to remain quiet and behave for the sake of the family where "we don't talk about such things." And so I kept quiet for the family. As if I owed them that. As if any victim of molestation should be compelled to pay that price or owes anyone that collateral. The same family that remains quiet to this day, the same family that encourages the continued silence. Silence, in turn, encourages behavior like Frankie's to continue. The f--king silence, long-embraced by my family. There will be no more silence for Tiny.

I experienced it again during the writing of this book. Nobody wanted to talk about it. Why do we have family relationships, then? What is family, if not a place to go to bare your soul and to find comfort in someone's willingness to listen? To my family: whether you know it or not, your silence is speaking for you, and it is speaking volumes.

One wonders how prevalent sexual abuse is. It's not just my family, after all; childhood sexual abuse isn't talked about anywhere. Children and adults who speak up about having been victimized rarely have any support. For a lot of reasons. None are good. None are justified. Most are based on the fear and shame of revealing the secrets of a trusted friend or family member. But there is shame, too, in revealing, if one eventually does, that one knew all along yet took so long to say something. A trusted friend or family member, by keeping quiet, must eventually recognize his or her own part in being duped, lied to, and manipulated, thereby having kept the abuse going. Who wants to allow that embarrassment to get out? It's selfish, arrogant, and prideful, but the silence continues until the person, who may well have once believed in good, lowers their own moral standards enough to fit in and become a part of the silence. Eventually, they will believe it is too late and not say anything.

But it is never too late. Not ever.

The recent "Me Too" movement has justifiably enabled women to come out about abuse at the hands of men, abuse often from years or even decades ago. I dream of a "Me Too" movement for men, especially men who were abused as boys. We've come to a point, it seems to me, where the reactions to these harrowing stories of abuse are now more positive. There is still an unfortunate train of thought that seeks to blame the victim. Child predators are often so skilled at hiding their crimes and portraying themselves as normal, kind people that there's a reluctance to believe accusations of abuse. The accuser must be in it for the money or for the attention. And besides, if it was really that bad, why did the accuser wait so long to say something? Now, with the "Me Too" movement, people are beginning to understand the dynamics behind the silence—the shame, the guilt, and the fear of public rebuke or even ridicule. Even suicide.

Of course I've understood this all along. Nevertheless, for my own prolonged silence, I stand here today ashamed, yet willing to take responsibility. Years went by as I kept trying to just *fit in,* to keep stuffing my own feelings of shame and guilt down the bottomless pit deep within the black hole that I fell into all those years ago. Until it all boiled over one night. If you are aware of sexual abuse in your family, on your block, in your church, in your school, for God's sake, be courageous like my wife Gina and say something early. If you are a survivor who has not been able to move beyond the pain of the abuse, now may be the time. Find some help. Help is out there, I promise you. In the appendix, you'll find a list of resources.

I won't pretend that I have all the answers. Your way of healing might end up being completely different from mine. But I do believe this: it's very difficult, if not impossible, to heal on your own. This is especially true if you are dealing with addiction issues. Seek professional help for those first. Take care of yourself physically, and then take care of your emotional issues. For both, seek professional help.

I often think of my mother's demons and I wonder at their cause. The promiscuity, the alcoholism, the anger, the self-loathing—from where did these come? Is it possible my mother was dealing, or, more accurately, not dealing, with her own shameful secret? Was there childhood sexual abuse in her past? Did she know of sexual abuse in the family? Did she know about her brother? Did she know of my abuse? This might explain a lot about her behavior. Whatever demons she had from her past, she spent her years trying to run from them, never confronting them. The running ultimately cost her her life.

There's a lesson there. A lesson that I hope might be taken by other members of my family, including my nephews who I know are dealing with their own demons, their own secrets. Whatever secrets the past holds, whether it's childhood sexual abuse or something else just as damaging, the secrets cannot be outrun. You'll have to find the path that works for you, but I believe that if you cry out to God, or Jesus, or the universe, or whatever higher power you believe in, your cries will be heard. For me, I have learned that my God is fair and just and knows our hearts. I trust Him. The right doors will appear and will open for you. Trust and you'll be led through them. Sometimes, I think the only reason I survived is because I cried enough. And screamed and whined. Even swore and shook my fist! Eventually, I was heard. And then *I* heard. You can be heard too. And then you will hear.

As for the sexual abuser, what can be done? Abusers are cunning, baffling, and deceptive. They are great manipulators, often playing dumb or innocent or both. They are master planners, setting up opportunities hours or days or even weeks in advance. They study the unknowing victim's movements, schedule, friends, and whereabouts. They coldly calculate. Once the abuse is known by others, the moral responsibility begins. Is enough being done? According to a report by the Washington State Institute for Public Policy, the average length of stay in prison is just forty-four months for those convicted of sex crimes against children. Astonishingly, this is less than the stay for those convicted of sexual crimes against adults, and pedophiles are notorious for recidivism. There is little contrition. Apologies and promises not to do it again are all part of the manipulative makeup of the pedophile. Jail terms need to be made longer, not as a deterrent, because nothing can deter the serial pedophile, but as a means to keep the pedophile from harming others.

In the end, as a society, supporting and encouraging the breaking of the silence remains our best defense against child sexual abuse. And if I've shared nothing else in this book, I hope I've conveyed how important it is to break the silence if you are a survivor who needs help. Say something to somebody. Scream it to them.

And then scream it to the heavens. Amazing things might just follow.

I only wish I'd have conveyed all of this earlier. I ran from it for nineteen years. Those years were followed by more years of AA, counseling, writing classes, and journaling. I had something to share, but then I found myself wanting to hide it away, wishing it would go away so that I wouldn't feel compelled to reveal my story publicly. Then in 2012, I blew out my knee and I had time to write about it some more. The writing started taking shape, and the wheels began to turn. But a few more years went by. Then, in July of 2015, I was told I needed a new aortic valve. Immediately. More free time on my hands. And the inner voice was getting stronger: *write the book*. Still, I had trouble putting it all in a readable, coherent format, breaking free of the running around in circles I was doing between my own ears.

During a regular morning swim workout in December of 2016, I experienced severe pain and numbness in my right arm. This resulted in another hospital visit, and this one finally convinced me that this book needed to be written. That it was no longer about me. That maybe my story could help someone else. Three days of hospital tests on my heart showed nothing, but nevertheless made me feel the urgency of getting my story out. An inner voice as strong—even stronger, perhaps—than that voice I'd heard running from Jon Maines in March of 1991 made it clear to me: Write the book. Yes, it'll be your name on it, but you are now on the other side of things and it's time to let it go. I listened to the voice. Through all of my pitfalls, stumbling blocks, insecurities, self-doubt, and the dreaded two-headed monster of shame and guilt, I finally moved beyond the feelings of complacency to do something in a positive way to heal.

It was not easy. Every chapter and every expense came with its own obstacles of fear and doubt. Several times I hit the wall. But somewhere in the process, I learned to trust, even more than I thought I was capable of. To truly let go, and let God help me. It's often been one step forward and two steps back. But each step forward was a huge accomplishment. I never knew when or if I would make it to the finish line. I just kept moving, kept persevering, kept praying. Upon hitting one wall, I often hit another, but I still kept moving. Not to move felt like I was dying, so moving, in and of itself, gave me a sense of accomplishment, even when, for the longest time, the finish line seemed invisible to me.

So if you're reading this and you're facing obstacles or maybe even a wall of your own, and you're stuck or full of fear, breathe. Try, first of all, to cause no more harm to yourself. Then find someone you can trust and confide in. Try to trust that person enough to help you find a counselor trained in helping to heal. We all deserve healing. We all deserve the gift of living in light and love. Like many abused people, you may be balancing the idea of speaking up with the desire to want to protect your family. Revealing your pain and suffering will upset the social apple cart. But accepting the suffering for some broader perceived "good" means carrying the burden alone. Worse, it means allowing the perpetrator to continue. Looking at it rationally, there's really not much to balance, is there? If you've gotten this far in life, you've absorbed enough pain to prove your toughness and resiliency. Now is the time to use that inner strength to break free. Find somebody with whom to share your burden. Seek help.

As for me, here it is (finally): *Tiny's Wall: A True Story of One Man's Battle to Overcome the Shame of Childhood Sexual Abuse.*

Here you go, Lord Jesus. And thank you.

—God bless,

*Fran Fidler*

**In Loving Memory Of**—Michael J. Flanagan, November 10, 1960 – January 10, 2017, my youngest brother.

**Dedicated To**—the love of my son Sam, my wife Gina, my sisters Kathy and Florence, my brothers Georgie, Jackie, and Danny.

With Thanksgiving and Love To—Margaret (Peg) "Gram" Robicheau, Mary Agnes "Great Grandma" Robicheau, Catherine Gorman "Nana" Fidler, Anne O'Connor, Mae Shepherd Wood, Kate Moore, Francis (Grampa) Robicheau, Hugh Fidler and Harry Kristy.

**In Prayer For**—Matthew and Michael, Cameron, Kasey, Michael Jr. and family everywhere. *For the wisdom to speak up, heal, and help others as you grow.*

**May God Bless All My Family, Friends, and Mentors**—a short list: Sean, Faithy, Henry, Vardaro, Marko, Jacko, and Dan; all my friends and teachers in Southie, The Boys & Girls Clubs, Miami and Naples, Florida; and a special thanks to the South Boston Boys Clubhouse and staff throughout my youth.

**In Gratitude**—this book would not have been possible without the support of:
My God whom I choose to call Jesus Christ
Pedro and Ann Wasmer
Jerry Moore
Bill and Janet Allyn
Micro Grants—Chuck and Arlene Garrity
Cover Photographer: Lou Hernandez Davila
Jenny and Karla Wheeler at Quality of Life Publishing Company
Jerry Payne, my editor, for your help with the words. A marathon-plus years later, here is our book to help others.
Jon Maines, 1991 arresting officer, for not shooting! And being a godly man and friend.
Thank you all.

# EPILOGUE

## MATTHEW 6:9-15

"This, then, is how you should pray: 'Our Father in heaven, hallowed be your name, your kingdom come, your will be done, on earth as it is in heaven. Give us today our daily bread. And forgive us our debts, as we also have forgiven our debtors. And lead us not into temptation, but deliver us from the evil one.' For if you forgive other people when they sin against you, your heavenly Father will also forgive you. But if you do not forgive others their sins, your Father will not forgive your sins."

# RESOURCES

Relevant facts for a better understanding:
*https://endsexualviolencect.org*
*https://www.fcasv.org/*
*https://1in6.org/get-information/myths/*
*https://www.malesurvivor.org/facts/*
*https://endsexualviolencect.org/resources/get-the-facts/male-survivors/*
*https://www.fcasv.org/sites/default/files/Male_Survivors_FS.pdf*
*https://forge-forward.org/wp-content/docs/female-perpetrators-and-male-victims-facts-and-resources.pdf*
*https://www.nsvrc.org/find-help*
*https://www.cachouston.org/child-sexual-abuse-facts/*

For direct help:
RAINN (Rape, Abuse, and Incest National Network: *www.rainn.org,* 800.656.HOPE (4673)
Childhelp USA: *www.childhelp.org,* 800.422.4453
National Domestic Violence/Abuse Hotline: *www.thehotline.org,* 800.799.7233

For counseling:
Sexual abuse counselors work in a variety of different settings throughout the community, including:
* Hospitals
* Rape crisis centers
* Domestic violence agencies and shelters
* Private practices
* Churches
* Correctional facilities

- Substance abuse and alcohol rehabilitation centers
- Child protective agencies
- Veterans and military hospitals
- Recovery meetings – attend, watch and listen to people tell their stories

# ABOUT THE AUTHOR

Fran Fidler grew up in the housing projects of South Boston, moving to Florida in 1986 in an attempt to escape the hidden shame and guilt of childhood sexual abuse. But Fran soon learned that there was no escape and that his past needed to be confronted. This realization put him on an arduous, ultimately triumphant process of healing. *Tiny's Wall: A True Story of One Man's Battle to Overcome the Shame of Childhood Sexual Abuse* is his story. A personal fitness trainer, Fran lives in Naples, Florida with his wife Gina. His son Sam graduated from Suffolk law school with his MBA in May of 2018, and recently passed the Florida Bar.

Frog Pond, Boston Commons

Made in the USA
Columbia, SC
27 March 2019